Solar System Gr. 2-4

Best Value Books™

Table of Contents

W9-AOF-106

ISBN 0-88724-445-9

About the book...

This book is just one in our Best Value™ series of reproducible, skill oriented activity books. Each book is developmentally appropriate and contains over 100 pages packed with educationally sound classroom-tested activities. Each book also contains free skill cards and resource pages filled with extended activity ideas.

The activities in this book have been developed to help students master the basic skills necessary to comprehend basic science facts about space. The activities have been sequenced to help insure successful completion of the assigned tasks, thus building positive self-esteem as well as the self-confidence students need to meet academic and social challenges.

The activities may be used by themselves, as supplemental activities, or as enrichment material for the science program.

Developed by teachers and tested by students, we never lost sight of the fact that if students don't stay motivated and involved, they will never truly grasp the skills being taught on a cognitive level.

About the author...

Barbara (Suzy) Notarianni, an elementary teacher for over twenty years, has taught in both public and private schools in three states. She has taught the solar system to fourth graders for the past six years, incorporating a hands-on approach to the learning process. Suzy believes that learning should be an interesting, fun, and creative process. She emphasizes full student participation and advocates group interaction for the implementation of lessons. Suzy has a Bachelor of Science degree and her Masters degree in Education.

Senior Editors: Patricia Pedigo and Roger De Santi
Production Director: Homer Desrochers
Production: Arlene Evitts and Debra Ollier

Ready-To-Use Ideas and Activities

The activities in this book will help children master the basic skills necessary to become competent learners. Remember, as you read through the activities listed below and as you go through this book, that all children learn at their own rate. Although repetition is important, it is critical that we never lose sight of the fact that it is equally important to build children's self-esteem and self-confidence if we want them to become successful learners.

Flashcard ideas

The back of this book has removable flash cards that will be great for basic skill and enrichment activities. Pull the flash cards out and cut them apart (if you have access to a paper cutter, use that). Following are several ideas for use of the flashcards.

• Help the student to learn to read the flash cards by flashing a few words at a time.

• Students may categorize the words into designated groups.

• The students may be allowed to create "open sorts", using their own ideas to create categories. (Ex: stars, planets, constellations, etc.)

• Keep a journal of the words and their definitions as they are introduced.

• Divide the cards into small groups and have children alphabetize them.

• Have students locate flash card words in books, magazines, and/or newspapers.

• Have a child select a number of words and write a paragraph that relates the words in a logical manner.

• Students can copy the flashcard words and their definitions into a journal as they demonstrate recognition and comprehension mastery.

• Have students illustrate the flash cards.

• Play "Bingo". Students select the words for their cards. Teacher gives the definition orally and students mark the words on their cards.

• Use the flashcards as key terms to outline each skill section as it is introduced.

• Use specific flashcard words as a guide for highlighting important information about any given skill section.

Suggested Classroom Activities

1. After presenting the information on stars and constellations, plan a visit to a planetarium.

2. Use the computer for bulletin board space news.

3. Choose a day of each week for "Space News". Share current space events.

4. Make a collage of pictures depicting space news and events.

5. Visit a space museum.

6. Get information about Space Camp from NASA.

7. Find out how the space program has benefitted man. Have students make a list of products developed by the space program that are a common part of our lives (i.e. velcro, microwaves, etc.).

8. Write letters to science fiction authors or screen play writers. Ask them how they create the setting for their space stories. (Is the story based on fact or completely imagined? Why were the authors interested in space? etc.)

9. Plan an exercise program that could be used in space. (The physical education teacher may help with this.)

10. Build a scale model of the shuttle.

11. Have students list songs that contain lyrics about space.

12. Write to NASA and find out the requirements for becoming an astronaut.

13. Chart the similarities and differences between astronauts and cosmonauts.

14. Hunt for micrometeorites by dragging a magnet through a container of rain water or snow. Scrape the magnet against a microscope slide and examine it to see if it picked up any micrometeorites.

15. Have groups of students become "advertising agencies" that promote travel to a particular planet, constellation, or other feature of space. See if they can "sell" their trip package to other students.

For More Information:

Aerospace Corporation
Attn: Office of Information
2350 E. El Segundo Blvd.
El Segundo, CA   90245

Aerospace Industries Association
1725 DeSales St., N.W.
Washington, DC   20036

American Map Company, Inc.
1962 Broadway
New York, NY   10023

American Society for Aerospace
Education
821 15th ST., N.W.
Washington, DC 20005

Astronomical Society of the Pacific
1290 24th Avenue
San Francisco, CA   94122

Civil Air Patrol
Attn: Aerospace Education and
Cadet Training
National Headquarters
Maxwell AFB, Al   36112

Hansen Planetarium Publications
15 South State Street
Salt Lake City, UT   84111

Jet Propulsion Laboratory
4800 Oak Grove Dr.
Pasadena, CA   91103

Lawrence Hall of Science
University of California
Berkeley, CA   94720

Martin Marietta
Denver Division, Box 179
12250 S. Highway 75
Denver, CO 80200

National Aerospace Education Association
Middle Tennessee State University
Box 59
Murfreesboro, TN   37130

National Geographic Educational Services
Dept. 76
P.O. Box 1640
Washington, DC   20013

Rand-McNally & Company
Box 7600
Chicago, IL   60680

Science Software Systems
11899 W. Pico Boulevard
West Los Angeles, CA 90064

Our Tour Guide

Before man could travel into space, scientists needed to know what safety measures needed to be taken. By sending animals into space first, we learned that the spacecraft must be airtight (let no outside air in). It must have plenty of oxygen, food and water. The spacecraft must have a radio to send information back to people on Earth. Scientists also learned that the spacecraft needed a heat shield to keep the animals inside from burning up when they returned to the Earth's atmosphere.

Many of the animals used in early space experiments were dogs. Scientists watched these animals closely to see how space travel might affect humans. Before long, scientists wanted to use animals that were a little more like humans. Small monkeys (and later, chimpanzees) were used for awhile.

One rhesus monkey was named Miss Baker. She was one of the first monkeys in space. She went up on May 28, 1959. After her space travel, Miss Baker spent her last twenty-five years at the Alabama Space and Rocket Center. This workbook is dedicated to Miss Baker because of the help she gave to the early space program.

Now Miss Baker will help you learn about space. She will take you through this book, showing you many of the things she has learned. Follow the maze through some of the sights and objects we will learn about on our "voyage" through this book.

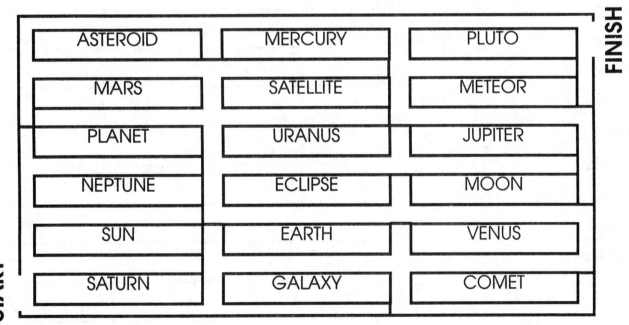

Name _____

Our Solar System

Miss Baker knows that we will learn more about space if we begin with our own solar system. The word "solar" means Sun. Our "solar system" is the Sun and all the things that orbit, or go around, it. There are nine known planets that orbit our Sun. Scientists think there may be more planets, but they have not proved it yet. Some of these planets have circles, or rings, around them. Most planets have a few satellites (moons) that orbit them as well. All of these things (the Sun, planets, and satellites) make up our solar system.

Below is a list of some of things we will learn about our Solar System. Put the words in alphabetical order.

	1. _____
	2. _____
Great Red Spot	3. _____
Pluto	4. _____
Uranus	5. _____
Earth	
Neptune	6. _____
Sun	7. _____
Moon	8. _____
Venus	
crater	9. _____
Jupiter	10. _____
orbit	11. _____
Mercury	12. _____
Saturn	
Mars	13. _____
satellite	14. _____
	15. _____

2

Name _____

What is the Name of the Largest Moon?

Write the answer to each clue on the blanks. Starting with the first box, write the boxed letters in order on the blanks at the bottom of the page.

1. Neptune's storm is called the _____ Dark Spot. ☐__ __ __ __

2. The seventh planet from the Sun. __ __ ☐ __ __ __

3. The twin planet to Uranus. ☐ __ __ __ __ __ __

4. The closest planet to the Sun. __ __ __ __ __ __ ☐

5. A satellite that circles the Earth. ☐ __ __ __

6. The largest of the planets. __ __ __ __ __ ☐ __

7. One of these on Earth is 23 hours and 56 minutes. ☐ __ __

8. The only planet with life. ☐ __ __ __ __

The name of the largest known moon anywhere (including other solar systems):

___ ___ ___ ___ ___ ___ ___ ___

Miss Baker's Graph of the Solar System

Miss Baker would like you to understand the distance between the planets and the sun. She has made the distance shorter to show you how the planets are related. Pretend that the graph of the football field on page 17 is outer space. The Sun rests in the bottom end zone. The planet distances are given below in yards. Answer the questions on this page, then fill in the graph. The first three planets have been done for you. When you have finished, you should be better able to imagine how far away Pluto is from the Sun!

	Number of Yards
Mercury	1
Venus	2
Earth	2 1/2
Mars	4
Jupiter	14
Saturn	24
Uranus	48
Neptune	74
Pluto	102

1. Which planet is the farthest from the Sun?

_____

2. Which planet is closest to the Sun?

_____

3. Which four planets are quite close together?

_____

4. Which planets are past the 50 yard line?

_____

5. Which two planets are only one yard apart?

_____

6. Which two planets are 24 yards apart?

_____

7. How many yards are between Pluto and Neptune?

_____

8. How many yards are between Jupiter and Saturn?

_____

9. How many yards are between Mars and Jupiter?

_____

Solar System Football Graph

Use the information given on page 15 to complete this graph.

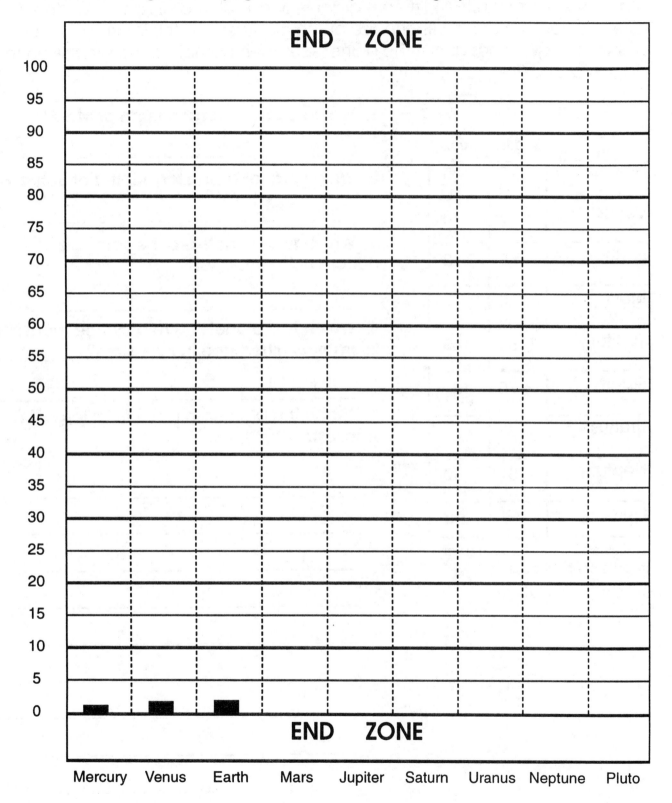

Miss Baker Compares the Planet Sizes

Miss Baker wants to see how the sizes of the nine planets compared to each other. She will make two different graphs, one in kilometers and the other in miles.   Below is a chart with the size of the planets. Use this information to answer the questions about the planet sizes then complete the graphs on the pages 19 and 20.

	mi.	km.
Mercury	3	5
Venus	8	12
Earth	8	12
Mars	4	7
Jupiter	89	143
Saturn	75	121
Uranus	32	51
Neptune	31	50
Pluto	1	2

* Miles and kilometers are given in units of one thousand.

1. Which planet is larger, Earth or Mars?

_____

2. Which planet is smaller, Jupiter or Saturn?

_____

3. Which two planets are the same size, according to this chart?

_____

4. Which two planets have only one thousand kilometers difference in their sizes?

_____

5. Name the planets in order from largest to smallest.

_____

_____

_____

_____

_____

_____

_____

Comparing Planet Sizes in Miles
(Size given in one thousand mile units)

Use the information given on page 18 to complete this graph.

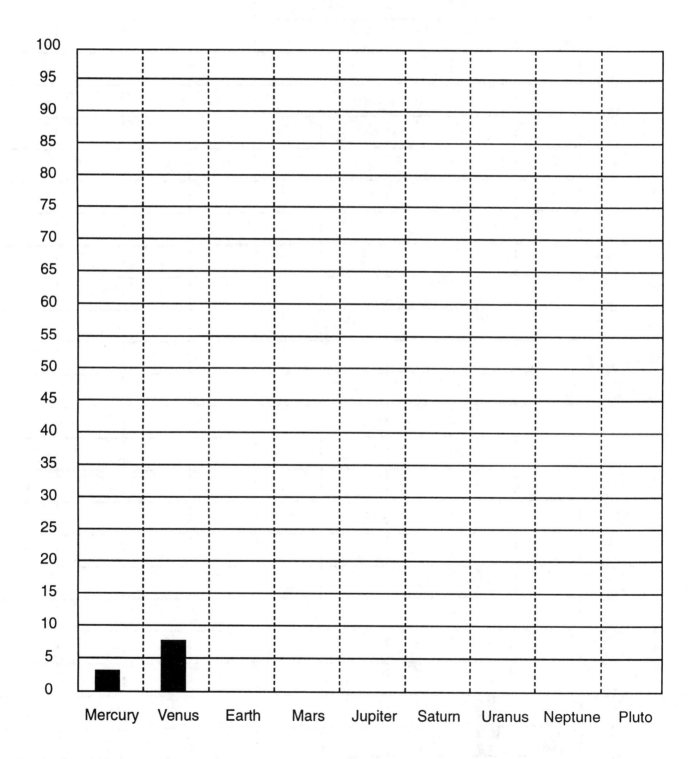

Comparing Planet Sizes in Kilometers
(Size given in one thousand kilometer units)
Use the information given on page 18 to complete this graph.

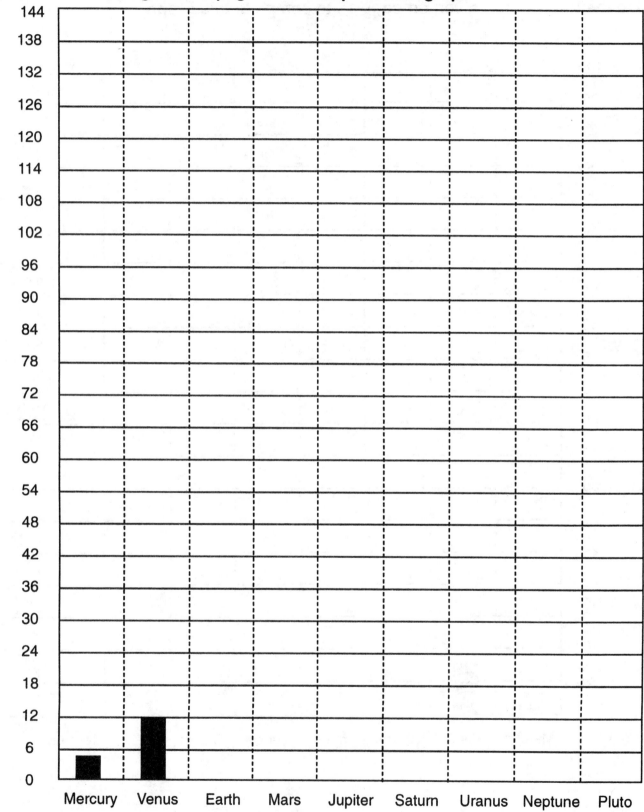

Comparing Planets

Use the information and the fact boxes from the sheets on each planet to answer the questions below.

1. Which planet is farther from the Sun: Mars or Venus?

_____

2. Which planet has a larger size: Neptune or Uranus?

_____

3. Which planet is an outer planet: Mars or Uranus?

_____

4. Which planet is closer to the Sun: Venus or Mercury?

_____

5. Which planet has more rings: Saturn or Jupiter?

_____

6. Which planet has fewer satellites: Earth or Uranus?

_____

7. Which planet has the shorter travel time (by jet) from Earth: Saturn or Mercury?

_____

8. Which planet has the shorter travel time (by rocket) from Earth: Jupiter or Venus?

_____

9. Which planet was named for the Greek god, Zeus: Neptune or Jupiter?

_____

10. Which planet has a hotter temperature: Venus or Pluto?

_____

Name _____

Comparing Planets

Use the information and the fact boxes from the sheets on each planet to answer the questions below.

1. Which planet is farther from the Sun: Jupiter or Saturn?

_____

2. Which planet is smaller in size: Earth or Pluto?

_____

3. Which planet is the fourth planet from the Sun: Jupiter or Mars?

_____

4. Which planet is an inner planet: Neptune or Venus?

_____

5. Which planet has more rings: Neptune or Uranus?

_____

6. Which planet has fewer satellites: Pluto or Mars?

_____

7. Which planet has the shorter travel time (by jet) from Earth: Mars or Venus?

_____

8. Which planet is an outer planet: Earth or Uranus?

_____

9. Which planet was named for the Greek goddess, Gaea: Mercury or Earth?

_____

10. Which planet was named for the Greek god, Apollo: Mercury or Mars?

_____

Name _____

Name the Mystery Planet

See how fast you can guess the mystery planet. Cover all the clues with another sheet of paper. Uncover the clues one at a time, read them, and write your "best guess" answer after each clue. You may not go back and change an answer once you have written it. At the end of the clues, look up the information about the planet you guessed last. Were you right? When you know the answer, write the name of the planet on the last line.

CLUES

1. I am an inner planet. _____

2. I am made of rock. _____

3. My size is about 7 thousand kilometers. _____

4. I have two moons. _____

5. There is a huge canyon on my surface. _____

6. I am often called the "Red Planet". _____

Draw the planet here and color it.

My name is _____.

Name the Mystery Planet

See how fast you can guess the mystery planet. Cover all the clues with another sheet of paper. Uncover the clues one at a time, read them, and write your "best guess" answer after each clue. You may not go back and change an answer once you have written it. At the end of the clues, look up the information about the planet you guessed last. Were you right? When you know the answer, write the name of the planet on the last line.

CLUES

1. I am an outer planet. _____

2. I have only one moon. _____

3. I was named after the Roman god of death. _____

4. I am made of frozen gas and water. _____

5. I am the smallest planet. _____

6. I am the ninth planet from the Sun. _____

Draw the planet here and color it.

My name is _____.

Create a Mystery Planet

Choose a planet. Use the information given on the planet worksheet to make up six clues about your planet. Start with difficult clues then make them easier as you go. Trade papers with a friend and see if you can solve each others mystery planet.

CLUES

1. _____

_____

2. _____

_____

3. _____

_____

4. _____

_____

5. _____

_____

6. _____

_____

Draw the planet here and color it.

My name is _____.

Rank the Planets

Use the information and fact boxes from the planet worksheets to put the planets in order each category.

DISTANCE FROM THE SUN (closest to the farthest)	**SIZE OF THE PLANET** (smallest to largest)
1. _____	1. _____
2. _____	2. _____
3. _____	3. _____
4. _____	4. _____
5. _____	5. _____
6. _____	6. _____
7. _____	7. _____
8. _____	8. _____
9. _____	9. _____

Name _____

Rank the Planets

Use the information and fact boxes from the planet worksheets to put the planets in order each category.

ALPHABETICAL ORDER

1. _____

2. _____

3. _____

4. _____

5. _____

6. _____

7. _____

8. _____

9. _____

ROTATION TIME
(length of one day)

1. _____

2. _____

3. _____

4. _____

5. _____

6. _____

7. _____

8. _____

9. _____

Grouping the Planets

Write the names of the planets that belong to each group.

INNER PLANETS

1. _____

2. _____

3. _____

4. _____

OUTER PLANETS

1. _____

2. _____

3. _____

4. _____

5. _____

ROCKY PLANETS

1. _____

2. _____

3. _____

4. _____

GAS PLANETS

1. _____

2. _____

3. _____

4. _____

5. _____

PLANETS WITH RINGS

1. _____

2. _____

3. _____

4. _____

PLANETS WITHOUT SATELLITES

1. _____

2. _____

TRUE OR FALSE

Read each sentence. Tell if the statement is true (T) or false (F).

_____ 1. Mars has three moons.

_____ 2. Caloris Basin, a large crater area, is found on Mercury.

_____ 3. The highest point on the Earth is the Dead Sea.

_____ 4. Jupiter is the fifth planet from the Sun.

_____ 5. Mercury has no satellites and no rings.

_____ 6. The Great Red Spot is found on Saturn.

_____ 7. Uranus has more satellites than any other planet.

_____ 8. Jupiter is the largest planet.

_____ 9. The length of a day on Mercury is just the same as on Earth.

_____10. It would take over 150 years to get to Saturn by jet.

_____11. Uranus is the third of the inner planets.

_____12. Mars is the only planet, other than Earth, that can support life.

_____13. Neptune was discovered by two astronomers in 1846.

_____14. Venus' surface cover is a pudding-like snow.

_____15. Pluto is the smallest planet.

_____16. Neptune is the coldest planet.

_____17. Saturn has more rings than any other planet.

_____18. Uranus was named for the Roman god of death.

CD-3727

Who am I?

Read each clue and decide who or what is the answer. Write your answer on the line. (Answers may be used more than once.)

1. Triton is one of my moons. _____

2. I have 8 rings and at least 24 satellites. _____

3. I have no rings and am the planet closest to the Sun. _____

4. I am usually the ninth planet (sometimes the eighth). _____

5. My surface is covered with a pudding-like snow. _____

6. I am very much like the Earth, but I have no water. _____

7. I am often called the "Red Planet". _____

8. I am the largest of all the planets. _____

9. I am the satellite that travels backwards around Neptune. _____

10. I am the only known planet with life. _____

11. I am the only satellite of Earth. _____

12. You can find the "Great Dark Spot" on my surface. _____

13. I am sometimes called the "Evening Star". _____

14. I was named for the Greek goddess, Aphrodite. _____

15. I am the only planet tipped completely on its side. _____

Plan Your Planetary Vacation

Miss Baker wants to help you plan a vacation to another planet. Name the **furthest** planet you can visit for each given time and type of transportation. The first one has been done for you.

TIME	TRANSPORTATION	PLANET
1. 4 years	rocket	_____
2. 691 years	jet	_____
3. 8 years	rocket	_____
4. 9 years	jet	_____
5. 17 years	rocket	_____
6. 11 years	jet	_____
7. 6 years	jet	_____
8. 3 months	rocket	_____
9. 2 years	rocket	_____
10. 514 years	jet	_____
11. 2 months	rocket	_____
12. 319 years	jet	_____
13. 75 years	jet	_____
14. 3 months	rocket	_____
15. 151 years	jet	_____

Postcards From Space

Miss Baker took a trip to several planets and their satellites in our solar system. She sent some postcards, but she forgot to tell what planet she was on! Help figure it out.

Read the postcards and look for clues. On the line, write the name of the planet or satellite that goes with the clues. Draw a picture of what Miss Baker saw.

Dear Class,

    I can't believe how much this planet looks like Earth. There are valleys, mountains, and even volcanoes. Yesterday was so hot because the clouds kept the heat close to the ground.

             Your friend,
             Miss Baker

PLACE: _____

Dear Class,

    I am so close to the Earth I can see the clouds, oceans, and continents. If I stayed here for 29 days, I would go all the way around the Earth one time. Oops, I almost stepped into a huge crater! I don't want to fall on this satellite, because I would really get dusty!

             Your friend,
             Miss Baker

PLACE: _____

Postcards From Space

Read the postcards and look for clues. On the line, write the name of the planet or satellite that goes with the clues. Draw a picture of what Miss Baker saw.

Dear Class,

   I can hardly believe it! I'm seeing the largest planet in our solar system! Hope I have time to visit all 16 moons and fly through its three rings!

            Your friend,
            Miss Baker

PLACE: _____

Dear Class,

   I am on the strangest planet. I've been told that there are 42 years of daylight then 42 years of night. I have been in the sun the whole week I've been here! I'm off to tour the 15 moons now.

            Your friend,
            Miss Baker

PLACE: _____

Dear Class,

   This planet is too hot during the day and freezing at night! There is the best view of the Sun from here, however. I'll be leaving here soon, just after I stop to see the Caloris Basin.

            Your friend,
            Miss Baker

PLACE: _____

Postcards From Space

Read the postcards and look for clues. On the line, write the name of the planet or satellite that goes with the clues. Draw a picture of what Miss Baker saw.

Dear Class,

    I am flying in the middle of a storm called the "Great Dark Spot". Boy is it dark! This storm is covers an area as large as the whole Earth. You have to come see this, but wear warm clothes!

               Your friend,
               Miss Baker

PLACE: _____

Dear Class,

    It has taken me over 16 years to get here, but I made it! I'm glad I brought my boots. This place has the weirdest snow I have ever seen. It feels just like pudding!

               Your friend,
               Miss Baker

PLACE: _____

Dear Class,

    I've never seen such wide rings before! I can fly over the rings, but I can't land on this gas planet. I plan to visit the 24 moons of this planet. I wonder if I'll have enough time to see them all.

               Your friend,
               Miss Baker

PLACE: _____

True or False

Read each sentence. Tell if the statement is true (T) or false (F).

_____ 1. Mars is further from the Sun than Earth.

_____ 2. The Earth orbits around the moon.

_____ 3. Neptune has a large moon called Saturn.

_____ 4. Mercury's path around the Sun sometimes causes it to be the eighth planet.

_____ 5. Saturn is the largest planet in our solar system.

_____ 6. The last planet in our solar system is Pluto.

_____ 7. Saturn takes 30 Earth years to go around the Sun.

_____ 8. Uranus, like Earth, has only one moon.

_____ 9. The Valles Marineris is found on Mars.

_____ 10. Saturn has more moons than any other planet.

_____ 11. Uranus is tipped over on one side.

_____ 12. The Earth has seven rings.

_____ 13. Jupiter is the largest planet in our solar system.

_____ 14. There are three stars in our solar system.

_____ 15. Mercury is the planet furthest from the Sun.

_____ 16. The Sun is made of iron and rock.

_____ 17. Neptune has 33 satellites.

_____ 18. Venus is the only other planet in our solar system that has life.

Name _____

True or False

Read each sentence. Tell if the statement is true (T) or false (F).

_____ 1. Pluto is a very rocky planet.

_____ 2. There is life on other planets.

_____ 3. Triton, the moon of Neptune, moves backwards.

_____ 4. There is no air, water, or life on the moon.

_____ 5. A day on Mars is shorter than a day on Earth.

_____ 6. Jupiter is a twin planet of Earth.

_____ 7. Venus is often called the Morning and Evening Star.

_____ 8. The Earth has only one moon.

_____ 9. Venus has thick clouds that keep it hot.

_____ 10. The highest point on Earth is the Dead Sea.

_____ 11. The Viking Lander 1 was the first spacecraft to land successfully on another planet.

_____ 12. Jupiter's "Great Red Spot" has been seen for over 300 years.

_____ 13. Saturn's rings are made of diamonds.

_____ 14. Neptune is a gas planet.

_____ 15. Earth is an outer planet.

_____ 16. Uranus was discovered by Sir William Herschel.

_____ 17. Jupiter has 3 rings and 16 moons.

_____ 18. Mars is also called the "Blue Planet".

Who Am I?

Read each clue and decide who or what is the answer. Write your answer on the line. (Answers may be used more than once.)

1. I am the planet closest to the Sun. _____

2. I am the planet that spins on my side. _____

3. I am the planet farthest from the Sun. _____

4. I am often called "the Red Planet". _____

5. I am the smallest planet. _____

6. I am a beautiful planet because my wide rings are very wide. _____

7. We are the two planet neighbors of Earth (the closest planets to Earth).

_____

8. I am the third planet from the Sun. _____

9. I am the number of planets in the solar system. _____

10. I am the number of satellites found around Neptune. _____

11. I am the seventh planet from the Sun. _____

12. I am usually the ninth planet. _____

13. I am the planet that has 3 rings and 16 satellites. _____

14. I am the planet with the most satellites. _____

15. I give light and heat to all the planets. _____

16. I am a body that orbits planets. _____

What Is A Star?

Why is it that Miss Baker can only see stars at night? During the daytime stars twinkle and shine, but they are hard to see. That is because another star, our Sun, is shining brightly on the Earth. At night, we are turned away from our Sun and can see the other stars better. Our night sky is filled with small spots of light, most of which are stars from our galaxy and others beyond ours. Each of these little spots of light is actually a burning ball of gas and dust, just like our Sun. They give off heat and light. A few of the "stars" are not really stars at all. They are planets that reflect the Sun's light (like a mirror) and just look like they are shining.

Miss Baker needs help. She wants to break the code and find out what makes a star so bright. Help her decode the message below.

A	B	C	D	E	F	G	H	I	J	K	L	M	N	O	P	Q	R	S	T	U	V	W	X	Y	Z
Z	Y	X	W	V	U	T	S	R	Q	P	O	N	M	L	K	J	I	H	G	F	E	D	C	B	A

____ ____ ____ ____ ____ ____ ____ ____ ____ ____ ____ ____
 Z   H   G   Z   I   R   H   Z   Y   Z   O   O

____ ____ ____ ____ ____ ____ ____ ____ ____ ____ ,
 L   U   S   B   W   I   L   T   V   M

____ ____ ____ ____ ____ ____ ____ , ____ ____ ____ ____   ____ ____ ____ ____
 S   V   O   R   F   N   Z   M   W   W   F   H   G

____ ____ ____ ____   ____ ____   ____ ____ ____ ____ ____ ____ ____ .
 G   S   Z   G   R   H   Y   F   I   M   R   M   T

It gives off ____ ____ ____ ____ **and** ____ ____ ____ ____ ____ .
                  S   V   Z   G   O   R   T   S   G

How Large Is A Star?

Miss Baker wants you to know that stars, like people, come in different sizes! Our Sun seems very large. It looks much larger than other stars because we are so close to it. The Sun also seems large because it is quite big. It would take over 100 Earths next to each other to fit across the center of the Sun! Although that size seems huge to us, our Sun is really only a medium (or middle) sized star! There are stars much smaller than the Sun. One small star named van Maanen's is about the same size as Mars. One of the largest stars is Betelgeuse. It is so enormous that our whole Solar System could fit inside it!

Use the information above to answer these questions.

1. **Are all stars the same size as our Sun?**_____

2. **Name a star that is smaller than our Sun:** _____

3. **Name a star that is larger than our Sun:** _____

4. **How many Earths would fit across the center of the Sun?** _____

5. **Is the Sun a small, medium, or large star?**_____

6. **Why does our Sun seem so huge to us?** _____

_____

Using the information from above, label these three stars: Sun, van Maanen, and Betelgeuse.

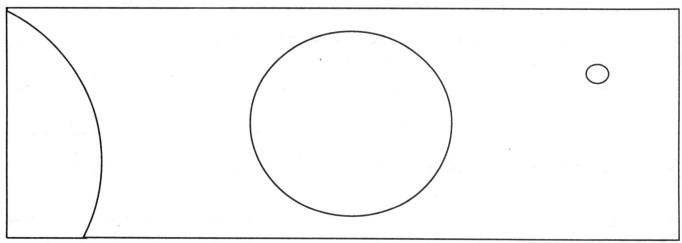

What Is The North Star?

If you were to stand on the North Pole and look straight up, you would see Polaris (also called the North Star).   As the Earth orbits the Sun, stars seem to "move" across the sky. The stars don't really move, we just see them from a different place in space. Polaris is the one star that is always in the same northern spot in our sky. For many years, sailors and hikers have used the North Star to help them figure out which direction they are traveling.   The North Star shines brightly in our night sky, even though it is very far away from earth. It is so far away that it takes 782 years for the the light from the North Star to reach Earth!

Answer the following questions.

1. What is another name for the North Star? _____

_____

2. Why do you think Polaris is called "the North Star" ?_____

_____

_____

3. How does the North Star help sailors and hikers?_____

_____

_____

4. Why do the other stars seem to move during the year? _____

_____

_____

5. How long does it take for the light from the North Star to reach the Earth?

_____

Our Sun Is A Star

The Earth is very close to a star. That star is called the Sun and is the center of our solar system. The Sun gives us the heat and light we need in order to live. The Sun is only a medium sized star, yet it would take one million Earths squeezed into a ball to equal the size of the Sun! The Sun is about five billion years old. Scientists believe that the Sun is half-way through its life and will burn for another five billion years or so. All of the energy of the Sun comes from gases that are burning in the core, or center. The energy is changed to heat and light as it reaches the surface of the Sun. The heat and light are radiated (given off) and travels through space to warm the Earth and give us light. On a hot summer day, the Sun may seem as if it is close enough to touch because it feels so hot. However, the Sun is really 150 million kilometers (93 million miles) away!

Use the information given above to answer these questions.

1. **What two things does the Sun give us?** _____

_____

2. **In what part of the sun is energy made?** _____

_____

3. **How old is the Sun?** _____

_____

4. **How far is the Earth from the Sun?** _____

_____

5. **How many Earths would it take to equal the size of the Sun?** _____

_____

6. **What happens to the Sun's energy as it reaches the surface of the Sun?**

_____

_____

_____

Sunspots

A few hundred years ago, a scientist noticed black spots on the surface of the Sun. These dark spots are called sunspots, but no one really knows what causes them. We do know that sunspots are the coolest places on the surface of the Sun (but even these spots are still too hot to go near). Sunspots can last for as short as a few hours or as long as a year! Scientists have noticed that sunspots usually come in groups. These groups return to the same places on the Sun about every eleven years.

To learn the name of the scientist and the year in which he discovered sunspots, solve the code below.

The name of the scientist is _____
17 11 22 19 22 15 25

He discovered sunspots in the year _____
AA FF AA BB

To see the sunspots, this scientist used a _____
30 15 22 15 29 13 25 26 15

When do sunspots return to the same place? _____
AA AA   35 15 11 28 29

11 = A	22 = L	33 = W
12 = B	23 = M	34 = X
13 = C	24 = N	35 = Y
14 = D	25 = O	36 = Z
15 = E	26 = P	AA = 1
16 = F	27 = Q	BB = 2
17 = G	28 = R	CC = 3
18 = H	29 = S	DD = 4
19 = I	30 = T	EE = 5
20 = J	31 = U	FF = 6
21 = K	32 = V	

Draw the Sun and a few sunspots:

Solar Prominences

Miss Baker thinks that solar prominences are really neat to watch. Solar prominences are streams of fire that shoot up from the surface of the Sun, turn, and loop back down again. Most solar prominences take about an hour from the start to finish, but some can last as long as several months. Our Sun may have many of these prominences on its surface at any given time. They can suddenly burst out of the Sun without warning. A solar prominence can shoot into the air as high as 41,700 km (25,000 mi) above the Sun!

Answer the questions below.

1. **What is a solar prominence?** _____

_____

2. **When can solar prominences happen?** _____

_____

3. **How high can a solar prominence travel above the Sun?** _____

_____

4. **How long do solar prominences last?** _____

_____

Draw a solar prominence on the Sun below.

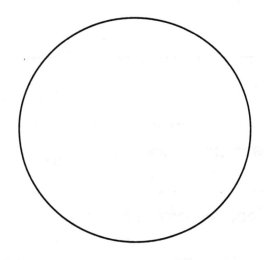

Solar Eclipses

Miss Baker couldn't believe her eyes! She was outside on a sunny day when the Sun disappeared! What Miss Baker was really seeing was a solar eclipse. A solar eclipse is when the moon comes between the Earth and the Sun, blocking out all its light. The shadow from the moon falls on the Earth and it becomes as dark as night in the middle of the day! The moon is not really as big as the Sun, but it looks like it is. That is because the Sun is so much farther away than the moon so they seem to be the same size when they are in the sky together. Sometimes the moon passes over part of the Sun. That is called a partial eclipse. When the moon covers the Sun completely, it is called a total eclipse. Although total eclipses are not rare, they can only be seen from the same spot on the Earth once every 400 years! (BE CAREFUL! NEVER look directly at the Sun, especially during a solar eclipse. The Sun's powerful rays could blind you.)

Below is a drawing of a solar eclipse. Label the Sun, Moon, and Earth then answer the questions.

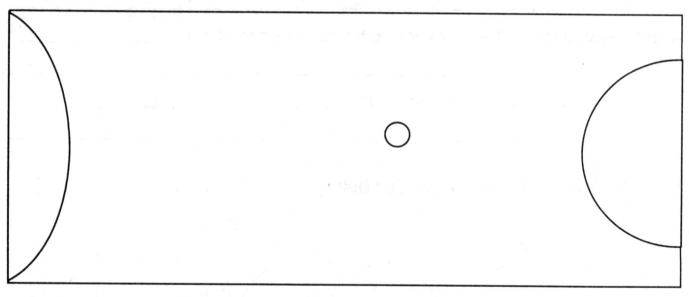

1. What is a solar eclipse? _____

_____

2. Why does the Earth become so dark? _____

_____

3. Why must you never look directly at the Sun? _____

_____

Star Struck

Miss Baker noticed that the "star" words have became jumbled in space. Help her to unscramble these words.

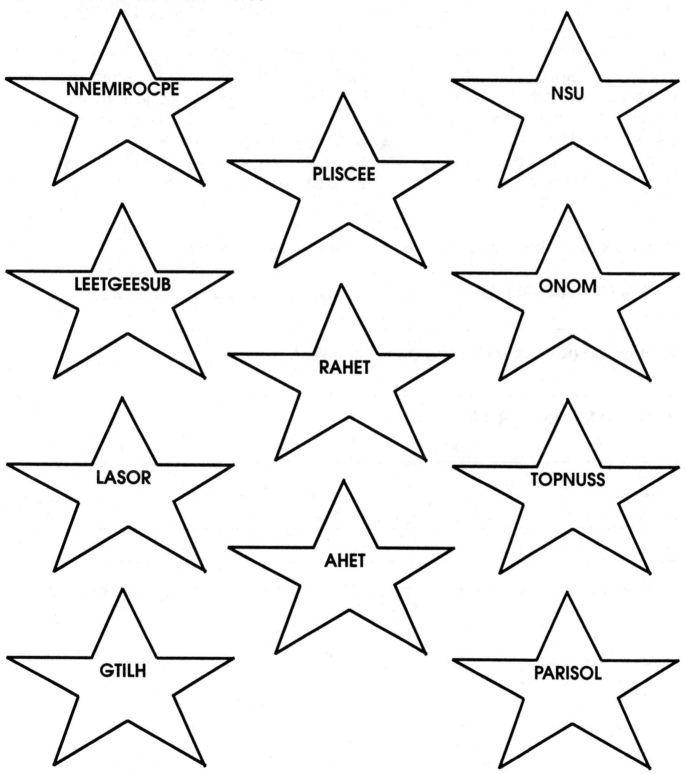

What Is A Constellation

Have you ever tried to count all the stars in the sky? If you could do it, you would probably count about 2,000 stars. Early scientists wanted to study the stars, but it was difficult to keep track of so many. They noticed that some of the stars were grouped together and looked like a picture. By playing "connect the dots" with the stars, scientists were able to make 88 pictures that used every star in the sky! These star "pictures" of people, animals, and things are called constellations. Ursa Major and Ursa Minor are constellations that look like bears. The constellation Leo looks like a lion while Draco becomes a dragon. Seeing the stars as part of a picture made it easier to find the stars scientists wanted to watch each night. People enjoyed the idea of constellations and made up many stories about these "star pictures" that are still told today.

Use the information given above to answer these questions.

1. **What is a constellation?** _____

_____

2. **How did early scientists use constellations?** _____

_____

3. **Name four constellations:**

_____

_____

_____

_____

4. **Connect the dots to see the constellation known as the "Big Dipper".**

WHAT IS A COMET?

Have you ever made a snowball with dust and ice? Probably not, but that is how a comet is formed. Comets are very much like dirty snowballs that travel in a long, narrow orbit around the Sun. As they come closer to the Sun, some of the ice melts and makes a sort of cloud (called the coma) of gas and dust around the snowball.   One strange fact about the comet is that its tail always points away from the Sun. As the comet comes toward the Sun, the tail is behind it. After the comet passes the Sun and is moving away, the tail is in front of it! Scientists think this might be caused by the strong solar winds from the Sun. These winds push the tail away, no matter which way the comet is headed.

Use the information above to answer these questions.

1. What is a comet? _____

_____

2. What makes a tail of a comet? _____

_____

3. What is unusual about the tail of a comet? _____

_____

_____

4. What do scientists think pushes the tail of the comet away from the Sun?

_____

5. Draw the tail of the comet below. (It is going toward the Sun.)

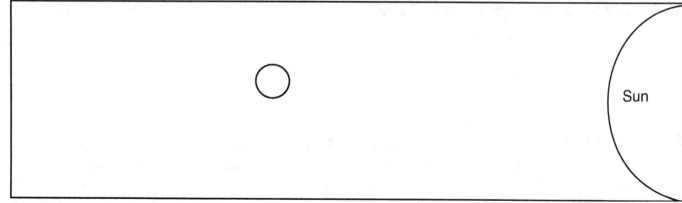

HALLEY'S COMET

What would you think if you saw a shiny ball with a long tail crossing the dark sky? That is what a comet looked like to people many years ago. They had no idea what comets really were. Maybe they thought a star had come loose and was flying through space! Comets are rare sights, and not many people have seen more than one in their entire life. In 1705, a scientist named Edmund Halley figured out how comets work. He studied a comet and realized that it was probably the same one the world had seen 76 years earlier. Halley gave us the idea that comets have orbits around the Sun, just like the planets. He predicted that his comet would return in 76 more years. Halley was right and his comet (since named Halley's Comet) returns to our part of space every 76 years!

Solve the following problems then crack the code to learn more about Halley's Comet.

●○ $8 + 8 - 3 + 5 - 9 - 1 =$ _____

✔ $16 + 3 - 5 + 6 - 10 + 2 - 11 =$ _____

✂ $4 + 3 - 2 + 7 - 6 + 3 - 9 =$ _____

✕ $5 + 4 + 3 - 2 + 6 - 10 =$ _____

✳ $2 + 3 - 1 + 5 - 2 + 5 - 3 =$ _____

☾ $10 - 2 + 5 + 4 - 2 - 1 - 10 =$ _____

☞ $7 + 1 - 4 + 8 + 2 - 6 + 2 - 8 =$ _____

✈ $12 + 3 - 2 + 5 - 10 - 5 =$ _____

1. **Halley's comet appeared in the year** ___ ___ ___ ___ **and was last seen**
                                                           ✔ ✳ ✔ ✂

    in ___ ___ ___ ___ .
        ✔ ✳ ●○ ✕

2. **It will return in** ___ ___ ___ ___ **and again in** ___ ___ ___ ___ .
                         ☞ ✂ ✕ ☞   ☞ ✔ ✈ ●○

       CD-3727

ASTEROIDS

Asteroids are pieces of rock and metal that orbit a star. Scientists believe asteroids may be pieces of planets that were never formed. Most of the asteroids in our solar system orbit the Sun in a belt between Mars and Jupiter. This group is called the Asteroid Belt. The asteroids in this belt range in size from 1 km (0.6 mi) to about 1000 km (600 mi) wide. The largest asteroid in this belt has been named Ceres and is 1038 km (623 mi) wide! A much smaller belt known as the Trojan group is much further away from the Sun. Some asteroids, like the small one named Icarus, orbit by themselves along their own path.

Break the code to find out more about the largest asteroid in the Asteroid Belt.

A	B	C	D	E	F	G	H	I	J	K	L	M	N	O	P	Q	R	S	T	U	V	W	X	Y	Z
Z	Y	X	W	V	U	T	S	R	Q	P	O	N	M	L	K	J	I	H	G	F	E	D	C	B	A

G S V   O Z I T V H G

Z H G V I L R W   R H

X V I V H .   R G   R H   Z H

O Z I T V   Z H   G S V

H G Z G V   L U   G V C Z H .

METEORITES

We saw a flash of light in the sky last night. It looked like a star that was falling to the ground. Miss Baker explained that bits of rock, metal, and dust called meteoroids are floating around in space. The Earth's gravity pulls these meteoroids into the Earth's atmosphere and they begin to burn as they fall to the ground. As they are burning they are called meteors. Most of the time meteors burn up completely as they fall. Sometimes, however, meteors will reach the ground. Then they are called meteorites. The Earth is hit by many meteorites every year. Most of them are so small no one ever notices. Some are very large, but they most of these have fallen in places where few people live. One of the largest meteorites ever found is as large as a car. It is kept in a museum in New York.

Fill in the blanks.

1. A meteoroid is _____

2. The Earth's _____ pulls meteoroids into our atmosphere where they begin to burn.

3. A burning meteoroid is called a _____

4. Most meteors burn up in the atmosphere. If they don't, they _____

_____

5. Most meteors _____ before they reach the ground.

6. When a meteor falls to the ground, it is then called a _____

_____

7. The Earth is hit by _____ meteorites every year, but most are never found.

8. One large meteorite can be found _____

_____

A SHOWER WITHOUT WATER?

Have you ever taken a shower without water? That would be hard to do, but there are showers without water. A meteor shower doesn't have any water. A meteor shower is when hundreds of meteors enter the Earth's atmosphere and fall burning through the sky like a shower of fire. These events happen every few years and are exciting to watch!

Use the code below to learn about a remarkable meteor shower that happened in 1966.

A	B	C	D	E	F	G	H	I	J	K	L	M	N	0	P	Q	R	S	T	U	V	W	X	Y	Z
10	20	30	40	50	60	70	80	90	15	25	35	45	55	65	75	85	95	16	17	18	19	1	2	3	4

___ ___ ___   ___ ___ ___ ___ ___ ___
17 80 50   35 50 65 55 90 40

___ ___ ___ ___ ___ ___   ___ ___ ___ ___ ___ ___
45 50 17 50 65 95   16 80 65 1   50 95

___ ___ ___   ___ ___ ___ ___   ___ ___ ___
80 10 40   65 19 50 95   65 55 50

___ ___ ___ ___ ___ ___ ___ ___
17 80 65 18 16 10 55 40

___ ___ ___ ___ ___ ___ ___   ___ ___ ___ ___ ___ ___ ___
45 50 17 50 65 95 16   20 18 95 55 90 55 70

___ ___ ___ ___ ___   ___ ___ ___ ___ ___ ___ .
50 19 50 95 3   16 50 30 65 55 40

                                CD-3727

A MIXED UP METEOR SHOWER

Miss Baker looked up in the sky one night and saw this strange meteor shower. Help her to arrange the words in the meteors to form a sentence that tells about a special meteorite.

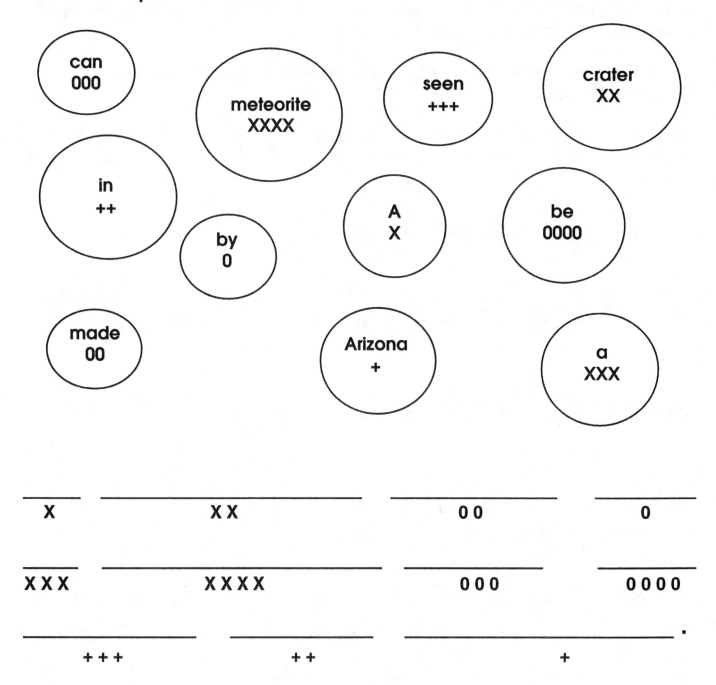

can
000

meteorite
XXXX

seen
+++

crater
XX

in
++

by
0

A
X

be
0000

made
00

Arizona
+

a
XXX

___ _____   0 0   0
X   X X

___ _____   000   0000
X X X   X X X X

_____ _____ _____.
+ + +   + +   +

This crater is 4,134 feet wide and 558 feet deep!

52   CD-3727

SCRAMBLED SENTENCES

Miss Baker was bringing you a group of sentences from outer space. Her spacecraft was hit by a meteor shower and the sentences got mixed up. Please help her to unscramble them so they make sense again.

1. Comet seen in be 2062 Halley's will again.

_____

_____

2. large of or metal rock are pieces Asteroids.

_____

_____

3. the Texas asteroid of is Ceres size An named.

_____

_____

4. no in meteor There is shower water a.

_____

_____

5. like dirty of ice ball a comet is A.

_____

_____

6. away faces from the comet tail The a Sun of always.

_____

_____

7. that make are groups stars Constellations pictures of.

_____

_____

Name _____   Skill: Celestial Bodies

A NEW WORLD

You have learned a lot about our Solar System. Wouldn't it be fun to discover a new one? Pretend that Miss Baker has taken you to a brand new solar system that is far beyond our own. The star is about the same size as our Sun, but this solar system has only three planets. As you travelled through the new solar system, you took notes about the planets (listed below). Use your notes to draw a picture of this solar system so the world can see what it looks like. You need to give a name to the system, its planets, and the moons.

My notes on the new solar system:

1. A middle sized star is the center of the solar system. It is yellow, like our Sun.

2. The planet closest to the star is the smallest. It is blue and has three smaller moons. All of the moons are grey and about the same size.

4. The second planet is blue and green. It looks as if it has land and water like the Earth does! This planet is larger than the first, but smaller than the third. It has two purple moons.

5. The third planet is the largest of the three. It is yellow and looks as if it may be made of gas. This planet also has three rings that circle it. The outer ring is orange, the middle ring is purple, and the inner ring is blue. This planet has no moons.

6. Name this new solar system:_____

7. Name the star: _____

8. Name each of the planets: _____

_____

_____

9. Name the five moons: _____

_____

_____

_____

_____

STAR WORDSEARCH

A	S	S	I	R	A	L	O	P	E	S	E
S	B	T	Q	W	Z	X	K	C	E	M	C
T	S	E	A	B	N	M	N	R	P	E	L
E	B	R	T	R	W	E	E	U	V	T	I
R	J	H	G	E	N	C	Y	J	K	E	P
O	S	D	F	I	L	Y	T	W	Q	O	S
I	B	V	M	R	Y	G	E	E	T	R	E
D	W	O	A	F	V	C	E	L	M	P	T
G	R	L	C	V	B	N	M	U	L	O	A
P	O	S	U	N	S	P	O	T	S	A	C
S	D	I	O	R	O	E	T	E	M	E	H
Y	U	X	E	T	I	R	O	E	T	E	M

Finds these words in the puzzle above. (They may go backwards!)

ASTEROID	**HALLEY**	**PROMINENCE**
BETELGEUSE	**METEOR**	**SOLAR**
CERES	**METEORITE**	**STAR**
COMET	**METEOROID**	**SUNSPOT**
ECLIPSE	**POLARIS**	

STAR CROSSWORD

56

ACROSS

1. A lot of meteors falling at once.

5. When the Sun gets blocked by the moon

9. A meteor that reaches the ground

10. A "dirty snowball" that orbits the Sun

DOWN

2. This man has a comet named after him

3. A dark spot on the Sun

4. Bits of rock or metal floating in space

6. A flame that loops from the Sun

7. Large pieces of rock or metal that orbit the Sun

8. A ball of burning gas that gives off heat and light

HUBBLE TELESCOPE

A telescope is an instrument that looks out into space and makes the planets, stars, and moons seem larger and closer to us than they really are. The Hubble telescope, which is named after Edwin Hubble, is the largest telescope of its kind. This telescope can see more stars than any telescope on earth. Why? It is not on the Earth, but is flying about 404 miles above the Earth as a satellite! The Hubble telescope is almost as large as a school bus with a mirror that is 8 feet across. The mirror acts as an "eye" for the telescope. There are also two cameras and special detectors that can see even the smallest source of light. It could see something as small as a flashlight on the Moon. The Hubble telescope satellite was built to last for years. When a problem arises that needs to be fixed, a space shuttle can be sent up to fix it!

Answer the following questions.

1. **What is the Hubble telescope?** _____
_____
_____

2. **Who was the telescope named for?** _____
_____
_____

3. **Why can the Hubble telescope see better than a telescope on Earth?**
_____
_____

4. **How many cameras does the Hubble telescope have?** _____
_____
_____

5. **How big is the mirror on this telescope?** _____
_____
_____

6. **How can this telescope be fixed if it breaks?** _____
_____
_____

Rockets Away

   Miss Baker was playing in the yard one day. She threw a ball up into the air. Almost right away, the ball fell back to Earth. Miss Baker knew that this was due to gravity, the force which holds us to Earth. How, then, can we launch rockets into space? Shouldn't they just fall right back to the Earth?

   Actually, in order for a rocket to fly into space, it must break the force of gravity. How can it do this? The answer is a speed of 40,000 kilometers per hour. If you could throw a ball this fast, it would go up in the sky and never return!

Follow Miss Baker in her rocket. Pick up the letter on each planet to form a sentence about space.

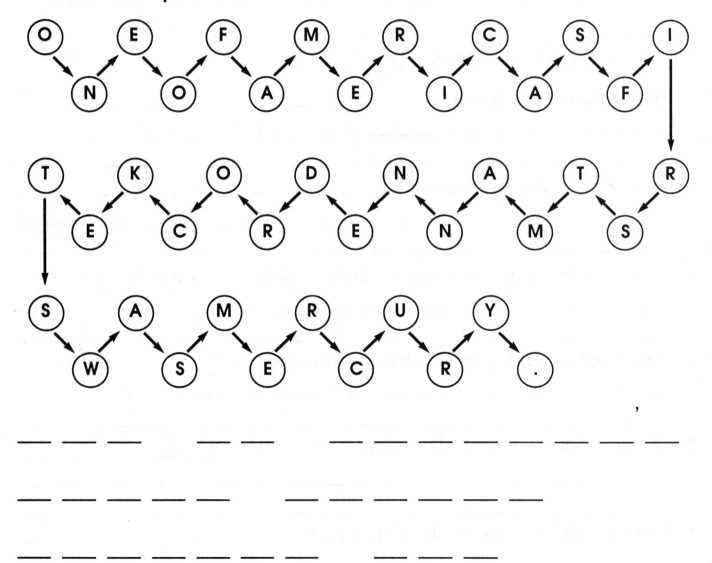

__ __ __   __ __ __ __ __ __ __ __

__ __ __ __ __   __ __ __ __ __

__ __ __ __ __ __   __ __ __

__ __ __ __ __ __ __ __ __

Rocket Math

Subtract the math problems below to find out about the first rockets.

23	15	39	24	18	50	16	40	79
- 13	- 7	- 25	- 7	- 9	- 34	- 7	- 29	- 67

41	62	25	67	36	49	20	39	54
- 28	- 39	- 8	- 48	- 18	- 25	- 9	- 27	- 34

58	44	25	30	31	91	59
- 38	- 26	-15	-15	- 19	- 69	- 38

8	9	10	11	12	13	14	15	16	17	18	19	20	21	22	23	24
H	A	C	D	E	G	I	K	M	N	O	P	R	S	T	U	W

___ ___ ___ ___ ___   ___ ___ ___ ___ ___

___ ___ ___ ___ ___ ___ ___ ___ ___ ___ ___

___ ___ ___ ___ ___ ___ ___ ___ ___ .

                   CD-3727

What Makes A Rocket Fly?

What makes a rocket move fast enough to break away from gravity? It needs energy, and lots of it. A car uses gas, or fuel, to give it energy. Your body uses food to make energy. A rocket needs fuel, too. The fuel tanks on a rocket hold liquid oxygen and hydrogen. When these two gases are mixed and burned, the fire and heat (energy) escapes from the bottom of the rocket. The energy that is made is strong enough to push the rocket away from the Earth. It goes right up through the atmosphere and into space! The gravity in space is not strong at all. Once the rocket is outside our atmosphere, it takes less fuel and energy to push the rocket where ever it is going.

Answer the questions below.

1. **What is made from fuel?** _____

2. **What type of fuel does a car use?** _____

3. **What fuel does your body use?** _____

4. **Name the two fuels used by rockets:** _____

_____

5. **What must be done with the two rocket fuels in order to make energy?**

_____

_____

6. **How does this large amount of energy help move a rocket?**

_____

_____

7. **Why does it take less energy to move a rocket once it is in space?**

_____

_____

Space Age Begins

In 1883, a Russian schoolteacher wrote a paper that explained how rockets could be made that would travel to space. For the next 25 years scientists tried to make such a rocket. In 1926 the first rocket was successfully launched. It only went 41 feet in the air (not even close to space). The importance of this rocket was in showing scientists that rockets really could fly. After that, several countries began a race for space. On October 4, 1957, the Soviet Union launched the first rocket to orbit the Earth. The name of the rocket was Sputnik. The space age had finally begun!

Circle every fourth letter and write it on the blanks below to discover the American who launched that first rocket.

W R T R G P L O B N M B W S A E Q

U I R X C Q T G I L G P Q Z O S Y

U D C W I D F D S A G H O R V R T

D V Z

The scientist's name :

___ ___ ___ ___ ___ ___   ___ ___ ___ ___ ___ ___ ___

Now unscramble some of the words in the following sentence to discover more about his experiment.

This <u>k c e r o t</u> _____ was launched with

liquid <u>l f e u</u> _____ . It only went up about

41 <u>e t e f</u> _____ into the in air. That was

enough to <u>v o p r e</u> _____ that rockets really could fly.

What Are Rocket Stages?

Rockets are spacecraft that are made up of stages (sections). Most of the rockets used for space travel have three stages. The first stage is full of fuel that is burned quickly during lift-off. This stage is jettisoned (dropped) as the rocket reaches the thin atmosphere near space. The second stage is also filled with fuel. This stage continues to push the rocket away from the Earth and is jettisoned when all the fuel has been burned. Stage two burns up as it drops back to the Earth. The third stage carries the payload (a satellite or a space capsule) into space and, finally, back to Earth. A capsule is a spacecraft where astronauts or cosmonauts sit. The first capsules had only one seat and were quite small. They were full of computers and equipment needed to control the spacecraft. Later capsules were larger and had room for three travelers.

Answer the following questions.

1. **What is another name for the stage of a rocket?**

_____

2. **How many stages do most rockets have?**

_____

3. **What is the purpose of the first stage (what does it do)?**

_____

4. **What is the purpose of the second stage?**

_____

5. **What happens to the first and second stages after all the fuel has been burned?**

_____

6. **What does the third stage carry?**

_____

7. **How are newer capsules different from the first ones that were used?**

_____

_____

The Space Shuttle

Miss Baker took us to see a very different spacecraft. It takes off like a rocket, orbits the Earth like a satellite, and comes back to Earth like an airplane. It is the space shuttle and it is the first spacecraft that can be used over and over. The space shuttle has four main parts: the orbiter, the two solid rocket boosters, the huge external fuel tank, and a set of three main engines at the bottom of the orbiter.

The two solid rocket boosters and the three main engines give the shuttle enough power to lift off the launch pad. The shuttle moves up through the atmosphere toward space. About two minutes after lift-off, the two boosters drop off and parachute back to Earth. They land in the ocean where they will be picked up by a ship. About six minutes later, the fuel in the external tank has been completely used. The external tank is also dropped into the ocean. The main engines are then used push the shuttle into orbit around the Earth. For the next few days the shuttle will orbit the Earth while the astronauts conduct experiments. When the astronauts are ready to return to Earth, the engines push the shuttle back into the Earth's atmosphere. Now the shuttle is flown much like an airplane as it lands on a runway.

Answer the following questions.

1. **Name the four parts of the space shuttle:**

_____

_____

_____

_____

2. **What makes the space shuttle different from other spacecraft?**

_____

3. **What happens to the two solid rocket boosters and the external fuel tank?**

_____

4. **Which part of the shuttle pushes it into orbit and back into the atmosphere?**

More About The Shuttle

Miss Baker took a tour of the space shuttle. She told us that this space-craft can hold up to ten people (usually four astronauts and six other passengers). The shuttle has a flight deck where the pilot sits to guide the craft. There is a crew cabin where the people eat and sleep. Behind the cabin is a large cargo bay that can carry up to 29,300 kg (65,000) pounds of equipment (payload). Sometimes a laboratory is put in the cargo bay. That is where the scientists perform many experiments. Trips on the space shuttle can last for two days to over two weeks.

Unscramble these sentences to learn more about the space shuttle.

1. is launched from The shuttle space Kennedy Space Center.

_____

_____

2. be 50 times can The space used shuttle between 100 and.

_____

_____

3. shuttle when in The orbit upside down it space flies is.

_____

_____

4. called The is Spacelab laboratory.

_____

_____

5. experiments do Mission lab specialists in the.

_____

_____

My Very Own

Miss Baker has invited us on a trip in the space shuttle. We will be gone for about two weeks. The shuttle has all the food, clothing, and bedding we will need for our trip, but you might want to bring along a few personal things. Perhaps you would like to have a favorite toy, family picture, or some things to experiment with in space. Miss Baker said there isn't a lot of extra room on the shuttle, so all your items must fit inside one small shoebox. The box should not weigh more than two pounds (4.5 kg).

Pack a small shoebox with the items you would like to take on this trip. When you are finished packing, compare your items with a buddy then answer the questions below.

1. What items did you bring?

_____

_____

_____

_____

_____

2. Choose two of your items and tell why you brought them.

_____

_____

_____

_____

_____

3. Did you and your buddy choose any items that were alike? If so, list them.

_____

_____

_____

Lift Off!

Miss Baker has asked us to take a trip on the space shuttle. First, we are strapped into our seats for take-off. The countdown begins: 10...9...8...7...6...5... 4...3...2...1... The two solid rocket boosters burn and push us upward. Lift-off takes place! After about two minutes the rocket boosters are used up and fall off the shuttle. Parachutes carry them down to the ocean so they can be picked up and reused another time. A few minutes later the fuel in the external tank is burned up. This tank is also dropped from the shuttle, but it cannot be reused. As it falls, it breaks into many pieces that fall into the ocean. Finally, the main engines push the orbiter into a path around the Earth. Now it is time to begin our space journey and start our experiments.

Solve the code to find the name of the first woman astronaut to ride the space shuttle.

15	19	23	28	31	35	38	45	49	55	59	63	69	73	78	82	89	99
P	Y	A	W	E	O	N	R	D	M	U	C	I	F	S	L	H	T

__99__ __89__ __31__   __73__ __69__ __45__ __78__ __99__   __28__ __35__ __55__ __23__ __38__

__23__ __78__ __99__ __45__ __35__ __38__ __23__ __59__ ____   to fly in the

__78__ __15__ __23__ __63__ __31__   __78__ __89__ __59__ __99__ __99__ __82__ __31__

__28__ __23__ __78__   __78__ __23__ __82__ __82__ __19__   __45__ __69__ __49__ __31__ .

The first woman astronaut to fly in the Space Shuttle was:

_____

Inside The Cabin

Miss Baker will show us cabin of the space shuttle. The cabin has three floors (decks). The lower deck has storage containers for things we might need on our flight. The mid deck is a room where we will spend most of our time. This room has a tiny kitchen called a galley where we can prepare our food. It also has bunk beds, lockers, and a restroom. From here we can climb a ladder to the top deck which is called the flight deck. This is where the commander and pilot sit to guide the shuttle. The flight deck is filled with instruments and controls. It also has a number of windows so we can see what is in front, next to, and above the shuttle!

Answer the questions below.

1. **How many levels are in the cabin?** _____
   Name them:

   _____

   _____

   _____

2. **What do you call the two crew officers that guide the space shuttle?**

   _____

2. **What is the name used for the kitchen on the space shuttle?**

   _____

3. **What will you find below the mid deck?**

   _____

4. **How do you get to the flight deck from the mid deck?**

   _____

5. **To which level would you go to get the best view of Earth?**

   _____

6. **On what level is the restroom found?**

   _____

I'm Floating!

After getting into orbit on the Space Shuttle, the first thing we notice is that Miss Baker is floating! So are we! There isn't enough gravity to hold us to the floor. We thought there was no gravity in space. Miss Baker told us that there is a tiny bit of gravity pulling on us, but it is so weak that it seems like there is none. This is called microgravity. Microgravity has some other affects on us as well. The blood in the lower part of our bodies now moves upward. We had to tighten our belts and shoelaces because our waists and feet are actually smaller in space! We are taller now, too. That is because there isn't as much gravity pulling against our backbones so they spread out a bit. Microgravity is a lot of fun!

To find out what else happens to your body in microgravity, unscramble the words below to make sentences.

1. feels a cold It getting like are you.

_____

_____

2. look eyes Your smaller.

_____

_____

3. dizzy and feel may You weak.

_____

_____

4. because muscles heart don't as work Your they hard weaken.

_____

_____

_____

5. disappear face on Wrinkles your.

_____

_____

Indoor Clothes

The first astronauts had to wear heavy spacesuits while they were orbiting the Earth. In the space shuttle we get to wear comfortable cotton pants and tops. It is very much like being on an airplane! The main difference is that our clothes have special pockets that close so that we can keep many items in them. If we don't put items in our pockets or attach them to the walls, they will float all over the cabin. We could get hit by a flying object!

To find the names of the items Miss Baker keeps in her pockets, unscramble the letters on each line. Use the clues to help you unscramble the letters.

1. Clue: I am full of ink and I help you write.
   P N E

   _____

2. Clue: I am filled with lead and I help you write.
   C L P N E I

   _____

3. Clue: I am a place where you keep important notes.
   A A D T   K O B O

   _____

4. Clue: You might wear me when we the Sun shines in the windows.
   N G S S S L U A E S

   _____

5. Clue: You might use me because you have the sniffles.
   S I T U S E

   _____

6. Clue: You use me when you need to cut something.
   C I S O S R S S

   _____

Outdoor Clothes

Miss Baker wants us to take a spacewalk outside. Before we can go, we must change into our spacesuit. Astronauts call this white suit an EMU (extrave-hicular mobility unit). Our EMU has three parts. The first part is the liner which looks like a pair of long johns. The liner has plastic tubes all through it to keep us cool or warm. Next comes our pressure vessel suit which includes our helmet and gloves. Finally, we put on our PLSS (primary life-supporting system). This looks like a backpack and has enough oxygen for seven hours! Ready?

Answer the questions below.

1. **What must we wear to take a spacewalk?**

_____

2. **What do the letters E.M.U. stand for?**

_____

3. **What do the letters P.L.S.S. stand for?**

_____

4. **What are the three parts of the spacesuit?**

_____

_____

_____

5. **What does the liner do?**

_____

_____

6. **Which part of the spacesuit has the helmet and gloves?**

_____

7. **Why is the backpack filled with oxygen?**

_____

_____

Let's Go!

Oh, dear! A part of the space shuttle needs to be repaired outside. You volunteer to go fix it. Miss Baker shows you into the airlock tunnel and closes the door. The door will keep oxygen in the cabin while you open the hatch to step into space.   In the airlock, you change into your EMU spacesuit. You will have to move around the outside of the spacecraft so you reach for your MMU (manned maneuvering unit). When you strap it on, the MMU allows you to fly without being attached to the space shuttle. Now you unlock the hatch to the outside. Wow! You're floating with the stars!

Solve the code to see what you will find inside your space helmet.

A	B	C	D	E	F	G	L	O	P	Q	R	S	T	U	V	W	X	Z
N	O	P	Q	R	S	T	U	M	W	C	I	H	F	L	D	E	B	A

Z   P Z G W E   G L X W '

T B B V '   O R Q E B C S B A W ,

W Z E C S B A W F '   Z A V Z

D - G R C   Z E W   T B L A V

R A   G S W   S W U O W G .

Eating In Space

It is your turn to fix dinner tonight on board the Space Shuttle. Miss Baker will show you where the galley (kitchen) is in the cabin. There you will find a pantry (to store food), oven, hot and cold water, and trays. Sorry, there is no refrigerator on board the shuttle! There are over 100 foods and 20 drinks to choose from. You really don't need to know how to cook. The food has been prepared and packaged to make it easier to fix. You will only need to heat the food or add water as directed on each package. Dinner should be ready in about 30 minutes!

Some of the foods you will find on board the Shuttle are listed below. Plan a meal (breakfast, lunch, dinner, or snack) for your crew . Draw your meal on the plate below. Label each item.

Broccoli au gratin   Mixed vegetables   Green beans   Asparagus   Tomatoes

Applesauce   Bananas   Pears   Pudding

Dried apricots   Dried peaches

Pecan cookies   Graham crackers

orange drink   Peanuts

punch   coffee

Tea   Cocoa

Ham   Bread

Turkey   Jam and jelly

Tuna fish   Peanut butter

Beef and gravy   BBQ Beef slices

Chicken a la king   Chicken and rice

Macaroni and cheese   Shrimp creole

Scrambled eggs   Cornflakes   instant breakfast (Chocolate or strawberry)

Why do you think milk and butter are not part of the list?

_____

Supper's On!

Guess what? Miss Baker tells us that we don't have to sit down for supper!
We can stand up, hang from the ceiling, or push ourselves into a corner. The
only rule is that we must be careful when we eat. Remember, food floats too!
We must avoid spills so that the food will not litter the cabin. Floating food may
get into some of the equipment and ruin it. Food that is left to float around
begins to spoil and cause germs that may make us all sick. We have a special
tray and a tiny spoon that helps us keep our food where it should be. Miss
Baker says that the small spoon grabs the food better. Some of our food can
be eaten right from the pouch it is packaged in. Eating in space is fun!

**Oh, no! Miss Baker spilled her water, cookies, popcorn, and peas.
Grab the pieces and unscramble them to make words that will complete
the sentences below.**

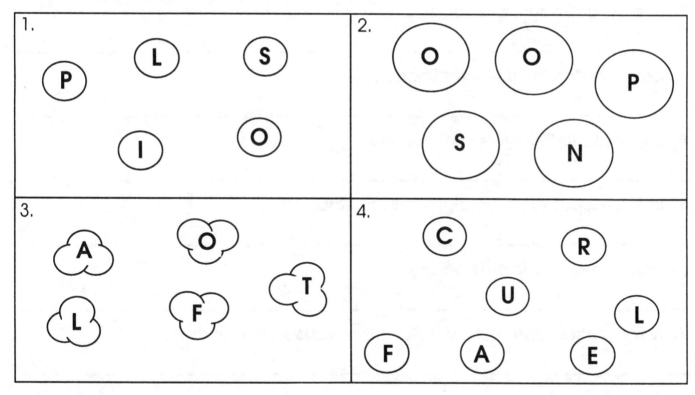

1. Floating food may _____ and cause germs.

2. Miss Baker uses a small_____ for eating.

3. Anything not tied or held down will _____ .

4. When eating in space, we must be very _____ .

Spacelab

Would you like to do any schoolwork in space? Miss Baker says that we can easily do science experiments during our flight. There is a big laboratory called Spacelab in the cargo bay! Ten countries worked together to build this flying laboratory so that experiments could be tested in space. In the lab we'll be able to grow crystals, test animals, look through special telescopes, and even take pictures of Earth. What do you want to do first?

To learn more about Spacelab, unscramble the words below to make sentences.

1. a in shuttle Spacelab is laboratory the.

_____

2. is in cargo Spacelab kept the bay.

_____

3. countries Ten build helped Spacelab.

_____

4. experiments Scientists in do lab the.

_____

5. in telescopes are special There Spacelab.

_____

6. can crystals We in grow space.

_____

7. have studied Spacelab and Scientists webs spiders in the.

_____

_____

8. pictures can take cameras of Special the Earth.

_____

_____

Keeping Fit

Miss Baker told us that microgravity makes it easy to move in space. Our muscles do not have to work as hard when we are aboard the shuttle. After Miss Baker's last trip into space her muscles were weak and it was hard to get used to the gravity back on Earth. Scientists have learned that it is very important for the space travelers to exercise every day so that their muscles will stay strong. There is a treadmill on board that works your muscles as if you are walking on Earth. This machine even slants upward so that you can feel like you are climbing a hill! You can work up a real sweat on this machine! In microgravity, the droplets will not run off your face like they do on Earth. When you get on the treadmill you must turn on a special vacuum air cleaner that will pull the water away from your skin. This way you can keep fit without getting soaked!

Answer the questions below.

1. **Why is it easier to move your body in space than on Earth?**

_____

2. **Why is it important that astronauts exercise while traveling in space?**

_____

3. **What piece of exercise equipment is on the Space Shuttle?**

_____

4. **Why does the treadmill slant?**

_____

5. **Why must you turn on an air cleaner before exercising?**

_____

6. **What other exercises do you think astronauts might do to keep their muscles in shape?**

_____

_____

Keeping Clean

At home you may take out the trash as a chore. In space, nothing can be thrown out because it would litter space. What will we do with our trash during our trip through space? All trash is sealed in plastic bags and put into a special storage container. We must be careful to clean the cabin every day so that germs will not spread and make us ill. We cannot take a shower or bath in space, but Miss Baker makes us wash our bodies with a wet cloth. After our wash, we will put on a clean shirt every three days and fresh pants once a week. Our dirty clothes are sealed in bags and stored in the same way as the trash. Don't forget to wipe off the food trays with a wet wipe after each meal. This keeps the trays clean and free of germs. There's a lot to keep clean in space!

Use the code to find the name of the trash or garbage sealed in each bag.

| A | C | D | E | F | H | I | L | M | N | O | P | R | S | T | U | W |

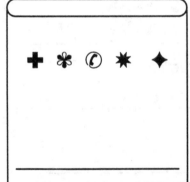

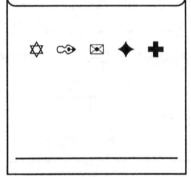

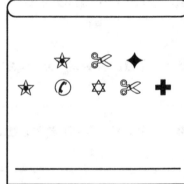

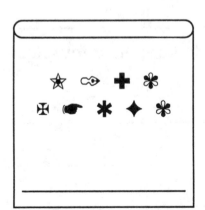

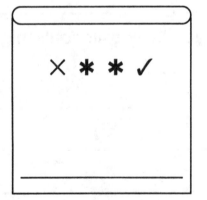

         CD-3727

A Mechanical Arm

Miss Baker tells us that there is a satellite in the cargo bay. We need to get it moved outside the shuttle so it can orbit the Earth. The satellite is very heavy. We know we won't be able to lift it by ourselves. What can we do? Our problem is solved when Miss Baker explains that the space shuttle has a RMS (remote manipulator system). The RMS is a mechanical "arm" with joints just like a real arm! It is able to lift and move things that weigh much more than a man or woman can lift. The controls for the RMS are on the flight deck. First one to the flight deck gets to move the satellite!

Break the code to find out how to operate the RMS.

1	2	3	4	5	6	7	8	9	10	11	12	13	14	15	16	17	18
A	C	D	E	F	G	H	I	L	K	M	N	O	P	R	S	T	U

$\overline{17}\ \overline{7}\ \overline{4}$ $\overline{2}\ \overline{13}\ \overline{12}\ \overline{17}\ \overline{15}\ \overline{13}\ \overline{9}$ $\overline{5}\ \overline{13}\ \overline{15}$

$\overline{17}\ \overline{7}\ \overline{4}$ $\overline{15}\ \overline{11}\ \overline{16}$ $\overline{8}\ \overline{16}$ $\overline{1}$

$\overline{2}\ \overline{13}\ \overline{11}\ \overline{14}\ \overline{18}\ \overline{17}\ \overline{4}\ \overline{15}$ $\overline{13}\ \overline{12}$ $\overline{17}\ \overline{7}\ \overline{4}$

$\overline{5}\ \overline{9}\ \overline{8}\ \overline{6}\ \overline{7}\ \overline{17}$ $\overline{3}\ \overline{4}\ \overline{2}\ \overline{10}$.

CD-3727

Feeling Ill?

Sometimes astronauts on board the space shuttle may need some medical attention. They may cut themselves or feel a little ill. The astronauts keep a SOMS (Shuttle Orbiter Medical System) on board. This is like a first-aid kit with a few extra items. The SOMS has a stethoscope (to listen to the heart), a blood pressure cuff, sutures to use as stitches, thermometers, bandages, tape, and medicines. The astronauts hope they will not need to use the SOMS, but they are glad to take it along just in case!

Read each statement. Decide which item from the SOMS kit you would use. .

1. Randy was opening a food pouch to have a quick snack. He was going to use his pocket knife to open the pouch. Just as Randy opened the knife, the shuttle was hit by a small meteoroid. The shuttle is fine, but Randy cut himself on the arm. The cut is not large, but it is deep and is bleeding a lot. Randy needs the SOMS kit. He would probably use the

_____

2. Sally has not gotten used to the microgravity yet. She feels a little sick to her stomach. She will get the SOMS kit and will take some

_____

3. Jamal's face looks red and he is sweating. He says he feels very hot. Jamal will need to take his temperature with a

_____

4. Kathy has just gotten off the treadmill. She may have overdone the exercise. She feels as though her heart is beating too fast. We can listen to her heartbeat with a

_____

What do the letters "SOMS" stand for?

_____

Time For Bed

It is been such a busy day that all of us are tired. Miss Baker asks us where we would like to sleep. There are several compartments that have a bunk bed. Each bunk has a mattress and pillow. There is also a reading light on the wall of each compartment. The bunk beds are comfortable, but it might be more fun to sleep on the floor or ceiling. Just be sure to attach the sleeping bag to something or you will float around the cabin as you sleep! Miss Baker tells us that getting enough sleep is just as important in space as it is on Earth. Remember to zip your arms inside the bag or strap them down. If you don't, you may wake up with your arms floating out in front of you!

Answer the following questions.

1. **Name three items that are built into the bunk bed compartments.**

_____

_____

_____

2. **If you don't care to sleep in a bunk bed, where else might you sleep?**

_____

3. **Why should you strap your arms down before you go to sleep?**

_____

Follow the steps in this long math problem to find out how often the Sun sets when you orbit the Earth in the shuttle.

1. **Write down the numeral 99** _____

2. **Subtract 12** _____

3. **Subtract 5** _____

4. **Subtract 32** _____

5. **Add 15** _____

6. **Subtract 20** _____

The sun sets every_____ **minutes when you orbit the Earth.**

Coming Home

The time has come for us to return to Earth. Miss Baker tells us that we must put everything we don't need into storage. Nothing can be left floating around the cabin. We need to bolt our seats to the floor and close the cargo bay doors. When everything is put away and fastened down, it is time to get into our antigravity suits. These suits help our bodies adjust as the gravitational pull becomes stronger. The shuttle is turned around so it will enter the Earth's atmosphere backwards. Heat proof tiles cover the shuttle so the friction and heat will not burn up the spacecraft as we come back into the atmosphere. Reentry is complete! The engines are slowed and the shuttle is turned back around. The shuttle is now flown like an airplane. We can see the runway straight ahead. We are home again!

Do you want to know how many heat proof tiles cover the space shuttle? Solve the math problems below. Use the answers to find the correct numbers and put the answers in the blanks at the bottom of the page.

$$
\begin{array}{r} 467 \\ -\ 135 \\ \hline \end{array}
\qquad
\begin{array}{r} 723 \\ -\ 471 \\ \hline \end{array}
\qquad
\begin{array}{r} 668 \\ +\ 122 \\ \hline \end{array}
\qquad
\begin{array}{r} 543 \\ +\ 261 \\ \hline \end{array}
\qquad
\begin{array}{r} 795 \\ -\ 494 \\ \hline \end{array}
$$

1. Find the digit that is in the tens place in the first problem. Write that number in the ten thousands place below.

2. Find the digit that is in the thousands place in the second problem. Write that number in the thousands place below.

3. Find the digit that is in the ones place in the third problem. Write that number in the hundreds place below.

4. Find the digit that is in the tens place in the fourth problem. Write that number in the tens place below.

5. Find the digit that is in the tens place in the fifth problem. Write that number in the ones place below.

The Space Shuttle has ____ ____ , ____ ____ ____ heat tiles.

Space Station

This afternoon Miss Baker told us about space stations. They are like cities that orbit the Earth. Space stations allow astronauts to stay in orbit for long periods of time. The Soviet Union set up one space station called Mir. A cosmonaut spent over a year there! A robot spacecraft (no people on board) brings fresh supplies and the mail from Earth to the space station. Other spacecraft can visit space stations when they need supplies. They can pick up food, water, and clean clothes at the space station.

Find out how many days the cosmonaut spent in space. Solve the math problems below then decode the message.

1. 20 x 2 =   + 1 =
2. 30 x 2 =   + 5 =
3. 10 + 15 =   + 5 =
4. 108 + 100 =   + 100 =
5. 40 + 40 =   + 15 =
6. 50 x 2 =   + 3 =
7. 44 + 40 =   + 4 =
8. 11 + 11 =   + 11 =
9. 30 + 40 =   +13 =
10. 50 + 40 =   + 7 =

1. Find the digit that is in the tens place in the first problem. Write that number in the hundreds place below.

2. Find the digit that is in the hundreds place in the fourth problem. Write that number in the tens place below.

3. Find the digit that is in the tens place in the tenth problem. Write that number in the ones place below.

The cosmonaut spent _____ _____ _____ **days in space.**

Talk Like An Astronaut

"Put on your EMU because NASA says we have EVA to do!" Astronauts use acronyms for many of the things they talk about. Acronyms are short words made from the first letters or syllables of two or more words that make up a phrase. For example, EMU stands for the longer phrase "extravehicular mobility unit". Below is a list of common acronyms that astronauts use and a description of what each means.

NASA	National Aeronautics and Space Administration (the name of the United States space program)
PLSS	Portable Life-Support System (a backpack filled with oxygen)
EMU	Extravehicular Mobility Unit (a spacesuit)
EVA	Extravehicular Activity (any work done outside cabin)
SOMS	Shuttle Orbiter Medical System (a medical kit)
STS	Space Transportation System (the shuttle, tank, and boosters)
KSC	Kennedy Space Center (a launch site in Florida)
SRB	Solid Rocket Booster (the first fuel stage of a shuttle)
IVA	Intravehicular Activity (any work done inside the cabin)
MCC	Mission Control Center (a place in Texas that watches and helps control all United States space flights)
WMC	Waste Management Compartment (the bathroom)

Can you talk like an astronaut? Choose five acronyms and write a sentence for each.

1. _____

_____

2. _____

_____

3. _____

_____

4. _____

_____

5. _____

_____

Design A Space Patch

   Every mission that is taken in space has a crew patch designed for it.
The patch gives the date, the name of the mission, and the names of the crew
members.

**Design the crew patch for the mission you went on with Miss Baker. Design
your patch on another piece of paper first. Copy it neatly into the circle below
then color it. Share your patch with the class.**

Space Exploration Crossword

ACROSS

1. Any body that orbits another body
3. The kitchen on a shuttle
5. A laboratory kept in the cargo bay
8. A space traveler trained in the United States
10. Name of the first dog in space

DOWN

1. It is worn outside the spacecraft
2. The feeling of having no weight
4. The first satellite to orbit Earth
6. A space traveler trained in the Soviet Union
7. A place on the shuttle to store payload
9. Primary life support system

Space Exploration Wordsearch

R	C	E	B	O	O	S	T	E	R	S	V
Q	O	O	M	L	A	U	N	C	H	K	E
S	S	B	S	U	W	Z	X	J	N	T	X
P	P	R	O	M	L	K	N	U	U	S	E
A	A	O	Q	T	O	O	B	A	W	H	R
C	C	C	Z	X	O	N	N	J	K	U	C
E	E	K	P	M	N	O	A	W	X	T	I
S	L	E	Q	I	R	G	F	U	D	T	S
U	A	T	B	T	R	H	O	U	T	L	E
I	B	A	S	E	A	R	T	H	E	E	Q
T	C	A	P	A	Y	L	O	A	D	L	W
M	I	C	R	O	G	R	A	V	I	T	Y

Find these words in the puzzle above:

ASTRONAUT	EMU	PAYLOAD
BOOSTERS	EXERCISE	ROBOT
BUNK	FUEL	ROCKET
CABIN	LAUNCH	SHUTTLE
COSMONAUT	MICROGRAVITY	SPACELAB
EARTH	MOON	SPACESUIT

 CD-3727

Secret Message

Add the problems and use the code to find out what the secret message is!

A	B	C	D	E	F	G	H	I	J	K	L	M
3	5	7	9	11	13	15	17	19	21	23	25	27

N	O	P	Q	R	S	T	U	V	W	X	Y	Z
2	4	6	8	10	12	14	16	18	20	22	24	26

—————————   ———————————————————————————————
7+7 8+9 6+5   6+6 10+7 9+7 6+8 12+2 12+13 4+7

—————————   ————————   ———————————————
4+3 1+2 1+1   3+2 3+8   8+8 5+7 2+9 3+6

————————   ———————————————————————
9+5 4+0   6+1 2+1 5+5 7+3 12+12

————————————————————————   ————————   ———————————————
2+5 0+3 2+8 13+2 1+3   5+9 0+4   1+2 2+0 3+6

———————————————————————   ———————————————————————
7+6 9+1 3+1 17+10   10+2 5+1 2+1 4+3 2+9

94   CD-3727

Space Word Syllables

Write the number of syllables in front of each "space" word.

_____ shuttle	_____ Jupiter
_____ orbiter	_____ meteor
_____ laboratory	_____ Mars
_____ satellite	_____ crystal
_____ runway	_____ medicine
_____ asteroid	_____ Spacelab
_____ comet	_____ experiment
_____ Earth	_____ moon
_____ planet	_____ Uranus
_____ telescope	_____ stage
_____ space	_____ scientist
_____ Mercury	_____ Venus
_____ Saturn	_____ Neptune
_____ Pluto	_____ exercise
_____ shuttle	_____ mission
_____ patch	_____ microgravity
_____ astronaut	_____ cosmonaut
_____ booster	_____ constellation
_____ flare	_____ prominence
_____ hydrogen	_____ helium
_____ eclipse	_____ sunspot
_____ star	_____ Halley
_____ dust	_____ crater
_____ rock	_____ gas
_____ solar	_____ rings

CD-3727

E.T.

There is no known life on any of the other eight planets in our solar system. There are millions of stars like our Sun in our galaxy. Perhaps there is another planet orbiting one of those stars that has life! The word "extraterrestrial" (the acronym is E.T.) means any unknown form of life. What do you think an E.T. might look like? Scientists sometimes use Latin words to name plants or animals. For example, a "monocornis" would be a one horned animal. The name helps to describe the animal.

Draw a picture of the E.T. named in each example. Use the list of Latin words to help you. Create your own E.T. and give it the proper Latin name. You can draw it on the back of this paper.

WORD	MEANING
mono	one
bi	two
tri	three
quadro	four
pento	five
ped	foot (feet)
cornis	horn
cephalus	head
milano	black
lenco	white
erythro	red
bruno	brown
lencus	line
punctata	dotted

Punctata quadroped bicephalus

Milanolencus Erythrocornis Triped

How Much Do You Remember?

Finish each statement or answer the question with a word or short answer.

1. Uranus was discovered in what year? _____

2. About how old is our Sun? _____

3. The planet closest to the Sun is _____ .

4. The EMU liner has _____ to help keep you cool.

5. Which planet has the most satellites? _____

6. An _____ occurs when the Moon comes between the Sun and Earth.

7. What is the distance to the Sun from Earth? _____

8. _____ is the planet closest to the Earth.

9. Which planet is known as Earth's sister planet? _____

10. A _____ is like a dirty ball of ice.

11. What comes near the Earth every 76 years? _____

12. _____ is another name for Polaris.

13. What is the name of the largest star? _____

14. How many stages do most rockets have? _____

15. The smallest and coldest planet is _____ .

16. On what planet will you find the Great Red Spot? _____

17. What is the name of Earth's satellite? _____

18. A group of stars that make a picture is called a _____ .

19. About how many food items are carried on the Shuttle? _____

20. About how many drink choices are carried on the Shuttle? _____

21. _____ makes you feel weightless.

22. Our Sun is a _____ sized star.

23. A _____ gives off light and heat.

24. The planet _____ is the only known planet with life.

25. _____ is the planet usually furthest from the Sun.

26. Triton is a moon of _____ .

27. The Caloris Basin can be found on _____ .

28. The _____ is a spacecraft that can be reused.

29. The planet _____ is also called the Evening Star.

30. The Great Dark Spot is found on the planet _____ .

31. A _____ is a Soviet Union person trained for space travel.

32. _____ is also called "The Red Planet".

33. The Great Red Spot is a _____ that is over 300 years old.

34. An _____ is a United States person trained for space travel.

35. _____ and _____ are the two gases found in a star.

36. Over 100 _____ fall to the ground on Earth each year.

37. The first man to step on the Moon was _____ .

38. The fifth planet from the Sun is _____ .

39. The planets are divided into inner and _____ .

40. _____ has more rings than any other planet.

41. Name the four main parts of the Space Shuttle.

    1. _____

    2. _____

    3. _____

    4. _____

42. _____ is a planet that is tipped on its side.

43. The Asteroid Belt orbits around the Sun between these two planets:

    1. _____

    2. _____

44. Dark spots on the Sun are called _____ .

45. When a meteor lands on Earth, it is called a _____ .

46. The kitchen on the space shuttle is called a _____ .

47. The first satellite to go into space was called _____ .

48. Mir is a Russian _____ .

49. Valentina Tereshkova was the first _____ in space.

50. In what year was the planet Neptune discovered? _____

51. A comet's tail always points _____ .

52. A solar _____ can loop as high as 25,000 miles from the surface of the Sun.

53. Our solar system is in what galaxy? _____

54. Valles Marineris is found on what planet? _____

55. _____ is the seventh planet from the Sun.

56. Many heat proof _____ line the space shuttle to keep it from burning up as it reenters Earth's atmosphere.

57. Burning _____ makes enough energy to lift a rocket through the atmosphere into space.

58. There are _____ levels or decks on a shuttle.

59. What was the name of the first dog in space? _____

60. Miss Baker was a _____ used in early space travel.

61. Which planet is between Jupiter and Uranus? _____

62. Venus is very hot during the day and very _____ at night.

63. It takes _____ years for the light from the North Star to reach Earth.

64. _____ was the scientist who used a telescope and discovered sunspots.

65. An eclipse happens when the _____ comes between the Sun and the Earth.

66. When the shuttle returns to Earth, it lands on a _____ .

67. How many people can the shuttle carry? _____

68. _____ is the largest planet.

69. The largest known asteroid is called _____ .

A Career In Space

Would you like to grow up to be an astronaut? There are several things you can do to prepare for being an astronaut. You must:

I. **Keep yourself in good physical condition. Exercise every day to make your muscles strong. Eat the proper foods to give your body energy.**

2. **Go to college. Graduate with a degree in engineering, science, or math.**

3. **Get an advanced degree (a masters or doctorate) or get a job in a space related field for at least three years.**

Would you like to know more about becoming an astronaut or other jobs in the space program? Write a letter to one of the addresses below and ask for information.

Astronaut Selection Office
Education
NASA
Johnson Space Center
Houston, TX 77058

American Society for Aerospace
821 15th Street, N.W.
Washington, D.C. 20005

Civil Air Patrol
Attn: Aerospace Education and Cadet Training
National Headquarters
Maxwell AFB, AL 36112

It is best to write your ideas and questions on a practice page before you write the letter. List your questions here to help you organize your thoughts. When you are finished, a parent or teacher can help you address and mail the letter.

_____

_____

_____

_____

_____

_____

Making A Comet

Miss Baker wants you to see what a comet looks like up close. Here is an experiment you can try with an adult.

Materials needed:
a large, open-mouthed pot
3 cups water
1 and 1/2 cups sand
a teaspoon of ammonia
rubber gloves
garbage bags
3 cups dry ice
a hammer or tool for pounding
a large metal spoon for stirring

1. Place garbage bag as a liner in the pot.

2. Put the water, sand, and ammonia into the pot and mix well.

3. ADULTS DO THIS! With rubber gloves on, wrap the dry ice inside several garbage bags.

4. With the hammer, smash the dry ice into small pieces.

5. Take 3 cups of this crushed dry ice and add to mixture in bowl.

6. Stir until almost frozen.

7. Lift the mixture inside the garbage bag from the pot.

8. With your gloved hands, shape the mixture into a ball.

9. Place the ball in a spot on the ground where everyone can see. DO NOT TOUCH!

10. As the dry ice changes into a gas, you will see trails of "smoke" coming from it. Pretend you are the solar wind and blow against the ball. Watch the tail form behind your "comet"!

Making Your Own Rocket

Would you like to see your own rocket travel through space? Try this experiment and you will see how rockets are pushed away from the Earth from the gas that escapes from the back of the rocket.

Materials needed:

12 feet (4 meters) of string
one large balloon
a clamp or clothespin
plastic drinking straw
masking tape.

1. Tie one end of the string to something heavy like a wooden chair or desk. This is your "launching pad".

2. Blow up the balloon. Clamp the stem of the balloon to hold in the air. The balloon will be your "rocket".

3. Cut the straw in half. Lay the two pieces end to end from the top of the balloon to the stem. Leave about an inch between the two pieces of straw. Use masking tape to attach the two sections of straw to the balloon. The straws will hold your "rocket" on course.

4. Start at the balloon stem and thread the loose end of the string through both sections of straw. Stretch the string out tightly and tie the end to another chair or heavy object. Make sure the string does not sag or touch the floor. The string will be the "orbit path" for your balloon.

5. Push the balloon back against the "launching pad". (Make sure that the balloon stem is facing the pad.) Now you are ready for lift-off.

6. Pull the clamp from the balloon stem! Zoom! The balloon will race to the other end of the string. Mission complete!

Tie another string along the same path and have race two balloons. See if the size of the balloon makes a difference in the speed at which it travels.

Growing Crystals

Astronauts have been experimenting with growing crystals in space. One thing they have found is that crystals can grow in space much faster than on Earth. A crystal is like a tiny brick that repeats itself in a pattern and grows. The "brick" comes in many different shapes like cubes, hexagons, or rectangles. Salt and sugar are common crystals that we use every day. Some gem stones such as quartz and amethyst are also crystals. You can grow your own crystals right here on Earth. They won't grow as fast as they do in space, so be patient!

Materials needed:
1 cup of very hot water
2 cups of sugar
1 pint jar
1 spoon
1 old towel
food coloring

1. **Pour the hot water into the pint jar.**

2. **Mix in half a cup of sugar. Stir it with the spoon until all the sugar dissolves (disappears into the water). Keep adding half a cup of sugar at a time and stir until all of the sugar has been dissolved (both cups).**

3. **Would you like to make colored crystals? Add one or two drops of food coloring to make the crystals blue, red, green, or yellow.**

4. **Wrap the towel around the jar. The towel helps hold in the heat so the solution will cool slowly. Crystals will form only if the solution cools *slowly*. Keep the towel wrapped around the jar and be patient!**

5. **Set the jar in a place where it will not be bumped or disturbed. (Movement will stop the crystals from growing.)**

6. **Leave the jar alone for two to three days. Groups of sugar crystals will form on the top and bottom of the jar. A few may even form along the sides.**

Super Achiever

_____

receives this award for

_____

Keep up the great work!

_____ _____

signed   date

Great Job!

_____

receives this award for

_____

Great Job!

_____ _____

signed   date

Certificate of Completion

_____

receives this award for outstanding performance in

_____

Congratulations!

_____   _____

signed   date

Solar System Award

_____

receives this award for

_____

You are terrific!

_____   _____

signed   date

Worksheet 1 — OUR TOUR GUIDE

Name _____   Skill: Planets

OUR TOUR GUIDE

Before man could travel into space, scientists needed to know what safety measures needed to be taken. By sending animals into space first, we learned that the spacecraft must be airtight (let no outside air in). It must have plenty of oxygen, food and water. The spacecraft must have a radio to send information back to people on Earth. Scientists also learned that the spacecraft needed a heat shield to keep the animals inside from burning up when they returned to the Earth's atmosphere.

Many of the animals used in early space experiments were dogs. Scientists watched these animals closely to see how space travel might affect humans. Before long, scientists wanted to use animals that were a little more like humans. Small monkeys (and later, chimpanzees) were used for awhile.

One rhesus monkey was named Miss Baker. She was one of the first monkeys in space. She went up on May 28, 1959. After her space travel, Miss Baker spent her last twenty-five years at the Alabama Space and Rocket Center. This workbook is dedicated to Miss Baker because of the help she gave to the early space program.

Now Miss Baker will help you learn about space. She will take you through this book, showing you many of the things she has learned. Follow the maze through some of the sights and objects we will learn about on our "voyage" through this book.

START		FINISH
ASTEROID	MERCURY	PLUTO
MARS	SATELLITE	METEOR
PLANET	URANUS	JUPITER
NEPTUNE	ECLIPSE	MOON
SUN	EARTH	VENUS
SATURN	GALAXY	COMET

© 1996 Kelley Wingate Publications   1   KW 1601

Worksheet 2 — Our Solar System

Name _____   Skill: Planets

Our Solar System

Miss Baker knows that we will learn more about space if we begin with our own solar system. The word "solar" means Sun. Our "solar system" is the Sun and all the things that orbit, or go around, it. There are nine known planets that orbit our Sun. Scientists think there may be more planets, but they have not proved it yet. Some of these planets have circles, or rings, around them. Most planets have a few satellites (moons) that orbit them as well. All of these things (the Sun, planets, and satellites) make up our solar system.

Below is a list of some of things we will learn about our Solar System. Put the words in alphabetical order.

Great Red Spot
Pluto
Uranus
Earth
Neptune
Sun
Moon
Venus
crater
Jupiter
orbit
Mercury
Saturn
Mars
satellite

1. crater
2. Earth
3. Great Red Spot
4. Jupiter
5. Mars
6. Mercury
7. Moon
8. Neptune
9. orbit
10. Pluto
11. satellite
12. Saturn
13. Sun
14. Uranus
15. Venus

© 1996 Kelley Wingate Publications   2   KW 1601

Worksheet 3 — Mercury

Name _____   Skill: Planets

Mercury

Mercury is the planet closest to the Sun and it is in the first position from the Sun. It is called an inner planet because it is some of the four planets closest to the Sun. Mercury is a rocky planet that looks a lot like our Moon with craters. Craters are formed from large pieces of rock, or meteors, crashing into the surface. One area where there are many craters is called Caloris Basin. There are no moons, or satellites, that orbit Mercury. Mercury gets very hot on its sunny side and very cold on its dark side. We could not live on Mercury.

FACT BOX
Distance from Sun: 57.8 million kilometers (36 million miles)
Rotation: 59 Earth days
Revolution: 88 Earth days
Diameter: 4,880 kilometers (3,030 miles)
Temperature: 350° C (660° F) day -170° C (-270° F) at night
Rings: none
Satellites: none
Travel time from Earth:
Jet: 10 years, 8 months
Rocket: 3 months
Light Years: 5 minutes
Named for: Roman god, Mercury (Greek god, Apollo)

Here is a code that Miss Baker found. Use it to fill in the letters on the secret message. The message will tell you the length of one day on Mercury.

(code box: A D E H R S T Y 6 7 1)

1 7 6   E A R T H   D A Y S

Look for the planet facts in the paragraph or fact box and fill in the answers.

1. Position of the planet: first
2. Size of the planet: 4880 kilometers 3030 miles
3. Number of rings: none
4. Number of satellites: none
5. Is it an inner or outer planet? inner
6. Give one interesting fact about the planet. crater - Caloris Basin (answers will vary)

© 1996 Kelley Wingate Publications   3   KW 1601

Worksheet 4 — Venus

Name _____   Skill: Planets

Venus

Venus is the second planet from the Sun and could almost be the sister planet to Earth. Venus and Earth are about the same size. Both planets are rocky, inner planets. Both planets have mountains, valleys, continents, and volcanoes. Venus, however, is covered with very thick clouds that trap the heat making it very hot. Venus is called the Morning Star and Evening Star because it is the brightest light in our sky at those times.

FACT BOX
Distance from Sun: 108 million kilometers (67 million miles)
Rotation: 243 Earth days
Revolution: 225 Earth days
Diameter: 12,100 kilometers (7,520 miles)
Temperature: 400° C (800° F)
Rings: none
Satellites: none
Travel time from Earth:
Jet: 5 years, 5 months
Rocket: 1.5 months
Light Years: 2.5 minutes
Named for: Roman goddess Venus (Greek goddess Aphrodite)

Complete the sentences below.

1. Venus is very hot because it is covered by thick clouds
2. Venus and Earth are almost the same size
3. Venus has these just like the Earth! mountains, valley, continent, or volcano
4. Venus has two nicknames: Morning Star Evening Star

Look for the planet facts in the paragraph or fact box and fill in the answers.

1. Position of the planet: second
2. Size of the planet: 12,100 kilometers 7520 miles
3. Number of rings: none
4. Number of satellites: none
5. Is it an inner or outer planet? inner
6. Give one interesting fact about the planet. sister planet to Earth (answers will vary)

© 1996 Kelley Wingate Publications   4   KW 1601

Answer Key

Name _____ **Skill: Planets**

EARTH

Earth is the third planet from the Sun. It is a rocky, inner planet. Earth is the only known planet with life. It is also the only planet with water. From space, we can see that there is more water on Earth than there is land. The Earth's land areas are divided into five continents. We have different seasons on Earth because the planet is tilted on its axis. Our Moon is the only satellite of Earth.

FACT BOX
Distance from Sun: 150 million kilometers (93 million miles)
Rotation: 23 hrs 56 min
Revolution: 365.3 days
Temperature: varies with location
Rings: none
Satellites: one (the Moon)
Travel time from Earth:
Jet:
Rocket:
Light Years:
Named for: Greek goddess Gaea, mother of the Titans

Directions: Break the code to find the highest and lowest points on Earth.

A B C D E F G H I J K L M N O P Q R S T U V W X Y Z
Z Y X W V U T S R Q P O N M L K J I H G F E D C B A

Highest point: **Mount Everest**
NLFMG VEVIVHG

Lowest point: **Dead Sea**
WVZW HVZ

Look for the planet facts in the paragraph or fact box and fill in the answers.

1. Position of the planet: **third**
2. Size of the planet: **12,800** kilometers **7900** miles
3. Number of rings: **none**
4. Number of satellites: **one**
5. Is it an inner or outer planet? **inner**
6. Give one interesting fact about the planet: **Only planet with life (answers will vary)**

© 1996 Kelley Wingate Publications 5 KW 1601

Name _____ **Skill: Planets**

Our Moon

Our moon travels around our Earth. It is a rocky body with no air, water, or life. The size of our moon is about the same size as the United States. The pulling force or gravity of the moon is much less than the Earth causing items to weigh less on the moon. If you weigh 60 pounds on Earth, you will only weigh 10 pounds on the moon! Our moon is covered with craters and is the only space body on which man has walked.

FACT BOX
Distance from Earth: 385,000 kilometers (239,000 miles)
Rotation: 27 days, 7 hrs, 43 mins
Revolution: 27 days, 7 hrs, 43 mins
Diameter: 3,476 kilometers (2160 miles)
Temperature: 130° C (266° F) day to -173° C (-280° F) at night
Rings: none
Satellites: none
Travel time from Earth:
Jet: 4 months
Rocket: 3 days
Light Years: 1.2 seconds

Add or subtract the following problems. Then match the answers with the letters. You will soon know the name of the first man on the moon!

$$\begin{array}{cccc} 26 & 7 & 16 & 12 \\ -2 & +8 & +3 & +10 \\ \hline 24 & 15 & 19 & 22 \\ N & E & I & L \end{array}$$

$$\begin{array}{ccccccccc} 9 & 39 & 45 & 22 & 20 & 59 & 12 & 67 & 38 \\ +2 & -11 & -22 & +7 & +10 & -31 & +13 & -43 & -21 \\ \hline 11 & 28 & 23 & 29 & 30 & 28 & 25 & 24 & 17 \\ A & R & M & S & T & R & O & N & G \end{array}$$

A = 11	E = 15	I = 19	M = 23	Q = 27	U = 31	Y = 35
B = 12	F = 16	J = 20	N = 24	R = 28	V = 32	Z = 36
C = 13	G = 17	K = 21	O = 25	S = 29	W = 33	
D = 14	H = 18	L = 22	P = 26	T = 30		

© 1996 Kelley Wingate Publications 6 KW 1601

Name _____ **Skill: Planets**

Mars

Mars is the fourth planet from the Sun. It is a rocky, inner planet. Mars is smaller and cooler than the Earth. It is sometimes called the "Red Planet" because it has a lot of iron in the soil. Mars has the highest mountain in our Solar System. It also has a very long valley, called Valles Marineris, that is as long as it is from the Atlantic Ocean to the Pacific Ocean as you cross the United States! Mars has two satellites, or moons.

FACT BOX
Distance from Sun: 227 million kilometers (140 million mi.)
Rotation: 24 hrs 40 mins.
Revolution: 687 Earth days
Diameter: 6,800 kilometers (4,200 miles)
Temperature: -23° C (-9° F) to 128° C (-199°F)
Rings: none
Satellites: 2
Travel time from Earth:
Jet: 8 years, 10 months
Rocket: 2.5 months
Light Years: 4 minutes
Named for: Roman god, Mars (Greek god Ares)

The American Viking Lander I was the first spacecraft to land successfully on another planet. Find the date of the Viking Lander I touchdown by answering the following questions:

1. Name the month that comes before August. **July**
2. Add the number of your fingers and toes together. **20**
3. Add the number of wheels on a car, a bicycle and a tricycle. Add ten more. **4 + 2 + 3 = 9 + 10 = 19**
4. Write the number for the word "seventy-six". **76**

The date was **July 20**, 19**76**

Look for the planet facts in the paragraph or fact box and fill in the answers.

1. Position of the planet: **fourth**
2. Size of the planet: **6800** kilometers **4200** miles
3. Number of rings: **0**
4. Number of satellites: **2**
5. Is it an inner or outer planet? **inner**
6. Give one interesting fact about the planet: **highest mountain (answers will vary)**

© 1996 Kelley Wingate Publications 7 KW 1601

Name _____ **Skill: Planets**

Jupiter

Jupiter is the fifth planet from the Sun. It is an outer planet made entirely out of gas. It has no solid surface. Jupiter is the largest planet in our Solar System. It would take over 300 Earths to fill Jupiter! Just above the surface of Jupiter is a huge storm that is almost twice as large as the Earth. This storm is called the Great Red Spot. There are three rings that circle Jupiter. It also has 16 moons!

FACT BOX
Distance from Sun: 778 million kilometers (480 million miles)
Rotation: 9 hrs. 55 min.
Revolution: 11.9 Earth yrs.
Diameter: 143,200 kilometers (89,000 miles)
Temperature: At the top of the cloud cover -130° C (-202° F)
Rings: 3
Satellites: 16
Travel time from Earth:
Jet: 74 years, 3 months
Rocket: 1 year, 9 months
Light Years: 35 minutes
Named for: Roman god, Jupiter (Greek god, Zeus)

Write the letter of the alphabet that comes **before** the given letter to discover more about Jupiter's huge storm.

THE GREAT RED
U I F   H S F B U   S F E

SPOT HAS BEEN
T Q P U   I B T   C F F O

SEEN FOR over 300 years!
T F F O   G P S

Look for the planet facts in the paragraph or fact box and fill in the answers.

1. Position of the planet: **fifth**
2. Size of the planet: **143,200** kilometers **89,000** miles
3. Number of rings: **3**
4. Number of satellites: **16**
5. Is it an inner or outer planet? **outer**
6. Give one interesting fact about the planet: **takes 300 Earths to equal the size (answers will vary)**

© 1996 Kelley Wingate Publications 8 KW 1601

Answer Key

SATURN

Saturn is the sixth planet from the Sun. It is an outer planet made of gas. Saturn is called a beautiful planet the rings that circle it. These rings are so wide they stretch as far as it is from the Earth to the Moon! Saturn also has 24 moons. That is more moons than any other planet! It takes Saturn almost 30 Earth years to go around the Sun.

FACT BOX
Distance from Sun: 1.4 billion kilometers (893 million miles)
Rotation: 10 hrs 40 mins
Revolution: 29 1/2 Earth yrs
Diameter: 120,600 kilometers (74,980 miles)
Temperature: At the top of the cloud cover -176° C(-285° F)
Rings: 8
Satellites: 24 known
Travel time from Earth:
Jet: 150 years, 5 months
Rocket: 3 years, 7 months
Light Years: 1 hr 11 mins
Named for: Roman god, Saturn (Greek god, Cronus)

Break the code to find more interesting facts about Saturn.

➡ ⟂ ✓ ⊗ ✱ ⚬ ➕ ⊡ ★
A C E G I K L N O R T

Saturn's largest moon is named **T R I T O N**

Saturn's rings are made of **R O C K** and **I C E** particles.

Saturn's rings were discovered by a scientist named **G A L I L E O**

Look for the planet facts in the paragraph or fact box and fill in the answers.

1. Position of the planet: **sixth**
2. Size of the planet: **120,600** kilometers **74,980** miles
3. Number of rings: **8**
4. Number of satellites: **24**
5. Is it an inner or outer planet? **outer**
6. Give one interesting fact about the planet. **has many rings (answers will vary)**

© 1996 Kelley Wingate Publications   9   KW 1601

Uranus

Uranus is the seventh planet from the Sun. It is an outer planet made of gas. The planet was discovered in 1781 by Sir William Herschel. Uranus is different from the other planets of of solar system because it is tipped on its side. This causes Uranus to spin differently from the other planets. Wind speed on Uranus can be as fast as 360 miles per hour. This planet has 11 narrow rings and 15 moons.

FACT BOX
Distance from Sun: 2.9 billion kilometers (1.8 billion miles)
Rotation: 17.3 hours
Revolution: 84 Earth years
Diameter: 51,100 kilometers (31,750 miles)
Temperature: -214 C (-353 F) at top of cloud cover
Rings: 11
Satellites: 15
Travel time from Earth:
Jet: 318 years, 6 months
Rocket: 7 years, 7 months
Light Years: 2 hrs, 30 mins
Named for: Roman god, Uranus

Tell if each statement is true (T) or false (F).

F 1. Uranus is an inner planet.
F 2. Uranus was discovered in 1871.
T 3. Uranus is tipped on its side.
F 4. There are 24 hours of daylight on Uranus.
T 5. Uranus has winds of over 360 miles per hour.
F 6. There are 15 rings and 11 moons for this planet.
T 7. Uranus is the seventh planet.
F 8. Uranus is a rocky planet.

Look for the planet facts in the paragraph or fact box and fill in the answers.

1. Position of the planet: **seventh**
2. Size of the planet: **51,100** kilometers **31,750** miles
3. Number of rings: **11**
4. Number of satellites: **15**
5. Is it an inner or outer planet? **outer**
6. Give one interesting fact about the planet. **tipped on side (answers will vary)**

© 1996 Kelley Wingate Publications   10   KW 1601

Neptune

Neptune is the eighth planet from the Sun. It is an outer planet and is made of gas. The planet was discovered in 1846 and is sometimes called the twin planet to Uranus. Neptune has a dark area on its surface that is about the size of Earth. Scientists believe it is a storm and have named it the "Great Dark Spot". This eighth planet also has eight moons. The largest moon is called Triton. It is really an unusual moon because it moves around Neptune backwards from all the other moons.

FACT BOX
Distance from Sun: 4.5 billion kilometers (2.8 billion mi)
Rotation: 16 hours
Revolution: 165 Earth years
Diameter: 49,500 kilometers (30,750 miles)
Temperature: -218 C (-360 F) at cloud cover
Rings: 5
Satellites: 8
Travel time from Earth:
Jet: 513 years, 2 months
Rocket: 12 years, 3 months
Light Years: 4 hrs, 2 mins
Named for: Roman god, Neptune (Greek god, Poseidon)

Answer the following questions.

1. Which other planet looks most like Neptune? **Uranus**
2. When was Neptune discovered? **1846**
3. What is the "Great Dark Spot"? **a large storm**
4. What is the name of Neptune's largest moon? **Triton**
5. How large is the "Great Dark Spot"? **size of Earth**
6. What is unusual about Triton? **moves backward**

Look for the planet facts in the paragraph or fact box and fill in the answers.

1. Position of the planet: **eighth**
2. Size of the planet: **49,500** kilometers **30,750** miles
3. Number of rings: **5**
4. Number of satellites: **8**
5. Is it an inner or outer planet? **outer**
6. Give one interesting fact about the planet. **storm called "Great Red Spot" (answer will vary)**

© 1996 Kelley Wingate Publications   11   KW 1601

Pluto

Pluto is usually the ninth planet from the Sun. It is an outer planet made of rock, gas, and water that have frozen into an unusual snow. Pluto is the last planet to be discovered and can only be seen with a very strong telescope. It is the smallest planet and is about the size of our moon. Pluto has a strange path around the Sun. Sometimes its orbit crosses in front of Neptune, and Pluto becomes the eighth planet for a few years!

FACT BOX
Distance from Sun: 5.9 billion kilometers (3.7 billion mi)
Rotation: 6 days, 9 hours
Revolution: 248 Earth years
Diameter: 2,300 kilometers (1,500 miles)
Temperature: -230° C (-382° F)
Rings: none
Satellites: 1
Travel time from Earth:
Jet: 690 years, 1 months
Rocket: 16 years, 5 months
Light Years: 5 hrs, 25 mins
Named for: Roman god, Pluto (God of death)

Solve each riddle.

1. To find the name of Pluto's moon:
   Write the word CUT **CUT**
   Add the word HARD **CUT HARD**
   Add the word ON **CUT HARD ON**
   Cross out the letters UTD **C͟U͟T͟HAR͟D͟ON**
   The word is **CHARON**

2. To step on Pluto's surface would feel like stepping into this:
   Write the word PUDDLE **PUDDLE**
   Add the word RING **PUDDLE RING**
   Cross out the letters L, E and R **PUDD͟L͟E͟ ͟R͟ING**
   The word is **PUDDING**

Look for the planet facts in the paragraph or fact box and fill in the answers.

1. Position of the planet: **ninth**
2. Size of the planet: **2300** kilometers **1500** miles
3. Number of rings: **0**
4. Number of satellites: **one**
5. Is it an inner or outer planet? **outer**
6. Give one interesting fact about the planet. **sometimes 8th planet (answers will vary)**

© 1996 Kelley Wingate Publications   12   KW 1601

Answer Key

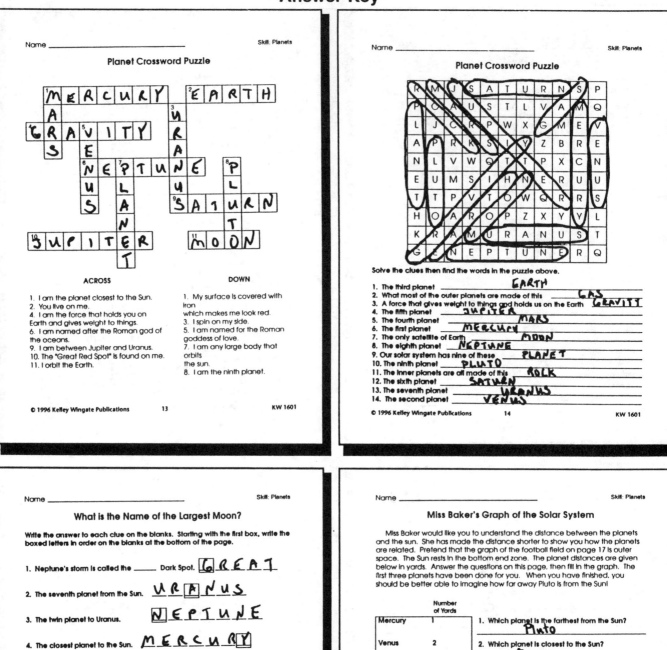

Page 13 — Planet Crossword Puzzle

ACROSS

1. I am the planet closest to the Sun.
2. You live on me.
4. I am the force that holds you on Earth and gives weight to things.
6. I am named after the Roman god of the oceans.
9. I am between Jupiter and Uranus.
10. The "Great Red Spot" is found on me.
11. I orbit the Earth.

DOWN

1. My surface is covered with iron which makes me look red.
3. I spin on my side.
5. I am named for the Roman goddess of love.
7. I am any large body that orbits the sun.
8. I am the ninth planet.

Crossword answers: MERCURY, EARTH, GRAVITY, NEPTUNE, SATURN, JUPITER, MOON, MARS, VENUS, URANUS, PLANET, PLUTO

© 1996 Kelley Wingate Publications   13   KW 1601

Page 14 — Planet Crossword Puzzle

Solve the clues then find the words in the puzzle above.

1. The third planet _____ EARTH
2. What most of the outer planets are made of this _____ GAS
3. A force that gives weight to things and holds us on the Earth _____ GRAVITY
4. The fifth planet _____ JUPITER
5. The fourth planet _____ MARS
6. The first planet _____ MERCURY
7. The only satellite of Earth _____ MOON
8. The eighth planet _____ NEPTUNE
9. Our solar system has nine of these _____ PLANET
10. The ninth planet _____ PLUTO
11. The inner planets are all made of this _____ ROCK
12. The sixth planet _____ SATURN
13. The seventh planet _____ URANUS
14. The second planet _____ VENUS

© 1996 Kelley Wingate Publications   14   KW 1601

Page 15 — What is the Name of the Largest Moon?

Write the answer to each clue on the blanks. Starting with the first box, write the boxed letters in order on the blanks at the bottom of the page.

1. Neptune's storm is called the _____ Dark Spot. GREAT
2. The seventh planet from the Sun. URANUS
3. The twin planet to Uranus. NEPTUNE
4. The closest planet to the Sun. MERCURY
5. A satellite that circles the Earth. MOON
6. The largest of the planets. JUPITER
7. One of these on Earth is 23 hours and 56 minutes. DAY
8. The only planet with life. EARTH

The name of the largest known moon anywhere (including other solar systems):

GANYMEDE

© 1996 Kelley Wingate Publications   15   KW 1601

Page 16 — Miss Baker's Graph of the Solar System

Miss Baker would like you to understand the distance between the planets and the sun. She has made the distance shorter to show you how the planets are related. Pretend that the graph of the football field on page 17 is outer space. The Sun rests in the bottom end zone. The planet distances are given below in yards. Answer the questions on this page, then fill in the graph. The first three planets have been done for you. When you have finished, you should be better able to imagine how far away Pluto is from the Sun!

	Number of Yards
Mercury	1
Venus	2
Earth	2 1/2
Mars	4
Jupiter	14
Saturn	24
Uranus	48
Neptune	74
Pluto	102

1. Which planet is the farthest from the Sun? Pluto
2. Which planet is closest to the Sun? Mercury
3. Which four planets are quite close together? Mercury, Venus, Earth, Mars
4. Which planets are past the 50 yard line? Neptune, Pluto
5. Which two planets are only one yard apart? Mercury and Venus
6. Which two planets are 24 yards apart? Saturn and Uranus
7. How many yards are between Pluto and Neptune? 28 yards
8. How many yards are between Jupiter and Saturn? 10 yards
9. How many yards are between Mars and Jupiter? 10 yards

© 1996 Kelley Wingate Publications   16   KW 1601

Answer Key

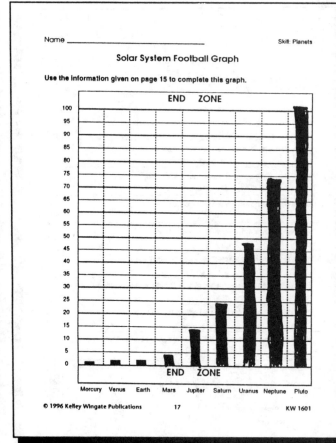

Solar System Football Graph

Use the information given on page 15 to complete this graph.

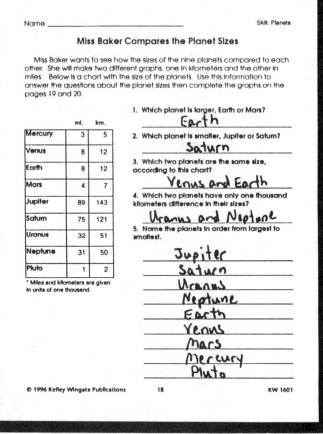

Miss Baker Compares the Planet Sizes

Miss Baker wants to see how the sizes of the nine planets compared to each other. She will make two different graphs, one in kilometers and the other in miles. Below is a chart with the size of the planets. Use this information to answer the questions about the planet sizes then complete the graphs on the pages 19 and 20.

	ml.	km.
Mercury	3	5
Venus	8	12
Earth	8	12
Mars	4	7
Jupiter	89	143
Saturn	75	121
Uranus	32	51
Neptune	31	50
Pluto	1	2

* Miles and kilometers are given in units of one thousand.

1. Which planet is larger, Earth or Mars?
   Earth
2. Which planet is smaller, Jupiter or Saturn?
   Saturn
3. Which two planets are the same size, according to this chart?
   Venus and Earth
4. Which two planets have only one thousand kilometers difference in their sizes?
   Uranus and Neptune
5. Name the planets in order from largest to smallest.
   Jupiter
   Saturn
   Uranus
   Neptune
   Earth
   Venus
   Mars
   Mercury
   Pluto

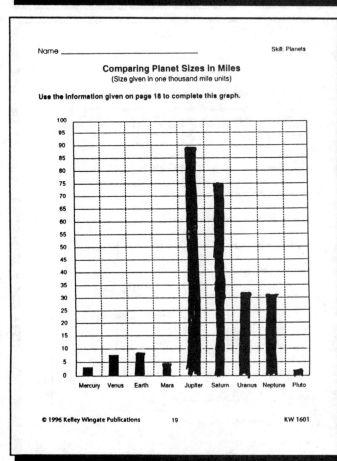

Comparing Planet Sizes in Miles
(Size given in one thousand mile units)

Use the information given on page 18 to complete this graph.

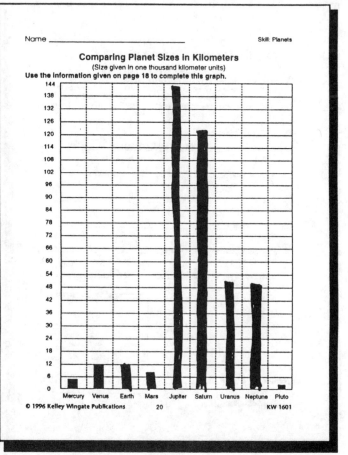

Comparing Planet Sizes in Kilometers
(Size given in one thousand kilometer units)

Use the information given on page 18 to complete this graph.

Answer Key

Name _____   Skill: Planets

Comparing Planets

Use the information and the fact boxes from the sheets on each planet to answer the questions below.

1. Which planet is farther from the Sun: Mars or Venus?
   _____ Mars _____

2. Which planet has a larger size: Neptune or Uranus?
   _____ Neptune _____

3. Which planet is an outer planet: Mars or Uranus?
   _____ Uranus _____

4. Which planet is closer to the Sun: Venus or Mercury?
   _____ Mercury _____

5. Which planet has more rings: Saturn or Jupiter?
   _____ Saturn _____

6. Which planet has fewer satellites: Earth or Uranus?
   _____ Earth _____

7. Which planet has the shorter travel time (by jet) from Earth: Saturn or Mercury?
   _____ Mercury _____

8. Which planet has the shorter travel time (by rocket) from Earth: Jupiter or Venus?
   _____ Venus _____

9. Which planet was named for the Greek god, Zeus: Neptune or Jupiter?
   _____ Jupiter _____

10. Which planet has a hotter temperature: Venus or Pluto?
    _____ Venus _____

© 1996 Kelley Wingate Publications   21   KW 1601

Name _____   Skill: Planets

Comparing Planets

Use the information and the fact boxes from the sheets on each planet to answer the questions below.

1. Which planet is farther from the Sun: Jupiter or Saturn?
   _____ Saturn _____

2. Which planet is smaller in size: Earth or Pluto?
   _____ Pluto _____

3. Which planet is the fourth planet from the Sun: Jupiter or Mars?
   _____ Mars _____

4. Which planet is an inner planet: Neptune or Venus?
   _____ Venus _____

5. Which planet has more rings: Neptune or Uranus?
   _____ Uranus _____

6. Which planet has fewer satellites: Pluto or Mars?
   _____ Pluto _____

7. Which planet has the shorter travel time (by jet) from Earth: Mars or Venus?
   _____ Venus _____

8. Which planet is an outer planet: Earth or Uranus?
   _____ Uranus _____

9. Which planet was named for the Greek goddess, Gaea: Mercury or Earth?
   _____ Earth _____

10. Which planet was named for the Greek god, Apollo: Mercury or Mars?
    _____ Mercury _____

© 1996 Kelley Wingate Publications   22   KW 1601

Name _____   Skill: Planets

Name the Mystery Planet

See how fast you can guess the mystery planet. Cover all the clues with another sheet of paper. Uncover the clues one at a time, read them, and write your "best guess" answer after each clue. You may not go back and change an answer once you have written it. At the end of the clues, look up the information about the planet you guessed last. Were you right? When you know the answer, write the name of the planet on the last line.

CLUES

1. I am an inner planet. _____ answers will vary _____

2. I am made of rock. _____

3. My size is about 7 thousand kilometers. _____

4. I have two moons. _____

5. There is a huge canyon on my surface. _____

6. I am often called the "Red Planet". _____ Mars _____

Draw the planet here and color it.

My name is _____ Mars _____.

© 1996 Kelley Wingate Publications   23   KW 1601

Name _____   Skill: Planets

Name the Mystery Planet

See how fast you can guess the mystery planet. Cover all the clues with another sheet of paper. Uncover the clues one at a time, read them, and write your "best guess" answer after each clue. You may not go back and change an answer once you have written it. At the end of the clues, look up the information about the planet you guessed last. Were you right? When you know the answer, write the name of the planet on the last line.

CLUES

1. I am an outer planet. _____ answers will vary _____

2. I have only one moon. _____

3. I was named after the Roman god of death. _____

4. I am made of frozen gas and water. _____

5. I am the smallest planet. _____

6. I am the ninth planet from the Sun. _____ Pluto _____

Draw the planet here and color it.

My name is _____ Pluto _____.

© 1996 Kelley Wingate Publications   24   KW 1601

Answer Key

Name _____   Skill: Planets

Create a Mystery Planet

Choose a planet. Use the information given on the planet worksheet to make up six clues about your planet. Start with difficult clues then make them easier as you go. Trade papers with a friend and see if you can solve each others mystery planet.

CLUES

1. _____ clues will vary _____

2. _____

3. _____

4. _____

5. _____

6. _____

Draw the planet here and color it.

My name is _answers will vary_.

© 1996 Kelley Wingate Publications   25   KW 1601

Name _____   Skill: Planets

Rank the Planets

Use the information and fact boxes from the planet worksheets to put the planets in order each category.

DISTANCE FROM THE SUN (closest to the farthest)	SIZE OF THE PLANET (smallest to largest)
1. Mercury	1. Pluto
2. Venus	2. Mercury
3. Earth	3. Mars
4. Mars	4. Venus
5. Jupiter	5. Earth
6. Saturn	6. Neptune
7. Uranus	7. Uranus
8. Neptune	8. Saturn
9. Pluto	9. Jupiter

© 1996 Kelley Wingate Publications   26   KW 1601

Name _____   Skill: Planets

Rank the Planets

Use the information and fact boxes from the planet worksheets to put the planets in order each category.

ALPHABETICAL ORDER	ROTATION TIME (length of one day)
1. Earth	1. Jupiter (10hrs)
2. Jupiter	2. Saturn (10.5 hrs)
3. Mars	3. Neptune (16 hrs.)
4. Mercury	4. Uranus (17 hrs.)
5. Neptune	5. Earth (24 hours)
6. Pluto	6. Mars (24.5 hrs.)
7. Saturn	7. Pluto (7 days)
8. Uranus	8. Mercury (59 days)
9. Venus	9. Venus (243 days)

© 1996 Kelley Wingate Publications   27   KW 1601

Name _____   Skill: Planets

Grouping the Planets

Write the names of the planets that belong to each group.

INNER PLANETS	OUTER PLANETS
1. Mercury	1. Jupiter
2. Venus	2. Saturn
3. Earth	3. Uranus
4. Mars	4. Neptune
	5. Pluto

ROCKY PLANETS	GAS PLANETS
1. Mercury	1. Jupiter
2. Venus	2. Saturn
3. Earth	3. Uranus
4. Mars	4. Neptune
	5. Pluto

PLANETS WITH RINGS	PLANETS WITHOUT SATELLITES
1. Jupiter	1. Mercury
2. Saturn	2. Venus
3. Uranus	
4. Neptune	

© 1996 Kelley Wingate Publications   28   KW 1601

TRUE OR FALSE

Name _____

Skill: Planets

Read each sentence. Tell if the statement is true (T) or false (F).

F 1. Mars has three moons.

T 2. Caloris Basin, a large crater area, is found on Mercury.

F 3. The highest point on the Earth is the Dead Sea.

T 4. Jupiter is the fifth planet from the Sun.

T 5. Mercury has no satellites and no rings.

F 6. The Great Red Spot is found on Saturn.

F 7. Uranus has more satellites than any other planet.

T 8. Jupiter is the largest planet.

F 9. The length of a day on Mercury is just the same as on Earth.

T 10. It would take over 150 years to get to Saturn by jet.

F 11. Uranus is the third of the inner planets.

F 12. Mars is the only planet, other than Earth, that can support life.

T 13. Neptune was discovered by two astronomers in 1846.

F 14. Venus' surface cover is a pudding-like snow.

T 15. Pluto is the smallest planet.

F 16. Neptune is the coldest planet.

F 17. Saturn has more rings than any other planet.

F 18. Uranus was named for the Roman god of death.

Who am I?

Name _____

Skill: Planets

Read each clue and decide who or what is the answer. Write your answer on the line. (Answers may be used more than once.)

1. Triton is one of my moons. **Neptune**

2. I have 8 rings and at least 24 satellites. **Saturn**

3. I have no rings and am the planet closest to the Sun. **Mercury**

4. I am usually the ninth planet (sometimes the eighth). **Pluto**

5. My surface is covered with a pudding-like snow. **Pluto**

6. I am very much like the Earth, but I have no water. **Venus**

7. I am often called the "Red Planet". **Mars**

8. I am the largest of all the planets. **Jupiter**

9. I am the satellite that travels backwards around Neptune. **Triton**

10. I am the only known planet with life. **Earth**

11. I am the only satellite of Earth. **Moon**

12. You can find the "Great Dark Spot" on my surface. **Uranus**

13. I am sometimes called the "Evening Star". **Venus**

14. I was named for the Greek goddess, Aphrodite. **Venus**

15. I am the only planet tipped completely on its side. **Uranus**

Plan Your Planetary Vacation

Name _____

Skill: Planets

Miss Baker wants to help you plan a vacation to another planet. Name the furthest planet you can visit for each given time and type of transportation. The first one has been done for you.

TIME	TRANSPORTATION	PLANET
1. 4 years	rocket	Saturn
2. 691 years	jet	Pluto
3. 8 years	rocket	Uranus
4. 9 years	jet	Mars
5. 17 years	rocket	Pluto
6. 11 years	jet	Mercury
7. 6 years	jet	Venus
8. 3 months	rocket	Mercury
9. 2 years	rocket	Jupiter
10. 514 years	jet	Neptune
11. 2 months	rocket	Venus
12. 319 years	jet	Uranus
13. 75 years	jet	Jupiter
14. 3 months	rocket	Mars
15. 151 years	jet	Saturn

Postcards From Space

Name _____

Skill: Planets

Miss Baker took a trip to several planets and their satellites in our solar system. She sent some postcards, but she forgot to tell what planet she was on! Help figure it out.

Read the postcards and look for clues. On the line, write the name of the planet or satellite that goes with the clues. Draw a picture of what Miss Baker saw.

Dear Class,

I can't believe how much this planet looks like Earth. There are valleys, mountains, and even volcanoes. Yesterday was so hot because the clouds kept the heat close to the ground.

Your friend,
Miss Baker

PLACE: **Venus**

Dear Class,

I am so close to the Earth I can see the clouds, oceans, and continents. If I stayed here for 29 days, I would go all the way around the Earth one time. Oops, I almost stepped into a huge crater! I don't want to fall on this satellite, because I would really get dusty!

Your friend,
Miss Baker

PLACE: **Moon**

Answer Key

Name _____   Skill: Planets

Postcards From Space

Read the postcards and look for clues. On the line, write the name of the planet or satellite that goes with the clues. Draw a picture of what Miss Baker saw.

PLACE: **Jupiter**

Dear Class,

I can hardly believe it! I'm seeing the largest planet in our solar system! Hope I have time to visit all 16 moons and fly through its three rings!

Your friend,
Miss Baker

PLACE: **Uranus**

Dear Class,

I am on the strangest planet. I've been told that there are 42 years of daylight then 42 years of night. I have been in the sun the whole week I've been here! I'm off to tour the 15 moons now.

Your friend,
Miss Baker

PLACE: **Mercury**

Dear Class,

This planet is too hot during the day and freezing at night! There is the best view of the Sun from here, however. I'll be leaving here soon, just after I stop to see the Caloris Basin.

Your friend,
Miss Baker

© 1996 Kelley Wingate Publications   33   KW 1601

Name _____   Skill: Planets

Postcards From Space

Read the postcards and look for clues. On the line, write the name of the planet or satellite that goes with the clues. Draw a picture of what Miss Baker saw.

PLACE: **Neptune**

Dear Class,

I am flying in the middle of a storm called the "Great Dark Spot". Boy is it dark! This storm is covers an area as large as the whole Earth. You have to come see this, but wear warm clothes!

Your friend,
Miss Baker

PLACE: **Pluto**

Dear Class,

It has taken me over 16 years to get here, but I made it! I'm glad I brought my boots. This place has the weirdest snow I have ever seen. It feels just like pudding!

Your friend,
Miss Baker

PLACE: **Saturn**

Dear Class,

I've never seen such wide rings before! I can fly over the rings, but I can't land on this gas planet. I plan to visit the 24 moons of this planet. I wonder if I'll have enough time to see them all.

Your friend,
Miss Baker

© 1996 Kelley Wingate Publications   34   KW 1601

Name _____   Skill: Planets

True or False

Read each sentence. Tell if the statement is true (T) or false (F).

T 1. Mars is further from the Sun than Earth.

F 2. The Earth orbits around the moon.

F 3. Neptune has a large moon called Saturn.

F 4. Mercury's path around the Sun sometimes causes it to be the eighth planet.

F 5. Saturn is the largest planet in our solar system.

T 6. The last planet in our solar system is Pluto.

T 7. Saturn takes 30 Earth years to go around the Sun.

F 8. Uranus, like Earth, has only one moon.

T 9. The Valles Marineris is found on Mars.

T 10. Saturn has more moons than any other planet.

T 11. Uranus is tipped over on one side.

F 12. The Earth has seven rings.

T 13. Jupiter is the largest planet in our solar system.

F 14. There are three stars in our solar system.

F 15. Mercury is the planet furthest from the Sun.

F 16. The Sun is made of iron and rock.

F 17. Neptune has 33 satellites.

F 18. Venus is the only other planet in our solar system that has life.

© 1996 Kelley Wingate Publications   35   KW 1601

Name _____   Skill: Planets

True or False

Read each sentence. Tell if the statement is true (T) or false (F).

F 1. Pluto is a very rocky planet.

F 2. There is life on other planets.

T 3. Triton, the moon of Neptune, moves backwards.

T 4. There is no air, water, or life on the moon.

F 5. A day on Mars is shorter than a day on Earth.

F 6. Jupiter is a twin planet of Earth.

T 7. Venus is often called the Morning and Evening Star.

T 8. The Earth has only one moon.

T 9. Venus has thick clouds that keep it hot.

F 10. The highest point on Earth is the Dead Sea.

T 11. The Viking Lander 1 was the first spacecraft to land successfully on another planet.

T 12. Jupiter's "Great Red Spot" has been seen for over 300 years.

F 13. Saturn's rings are made of diamonds.

T 14. Neptune is a gas planet.

F 15. Earth is an outer planet.

T 16. Uranus was discovered by Sir William Herschel.

T 17. Jupiter has 3 rings and 16 moons.

F 18. Mars is also called the "Blue Planet".

© 1996 Kelley Wingate Publications   36   KW 1601

© 1996 Kelley Wingate Publications   115   CD-3727

Answer Key

Name _____
Skill: Planets

Who Am I?

Read each clue and decide who or what is the answer. Write your answer on the line. (Answers may be used more than once.)

1. I am the planet closest to the Sun. **Mercury**

2. I am the planet that spins on my side. **Uranus**

3. I am the planet farthest from the Sun. **Pluto**

4. I am often called "the Red Planet". **Mars**

5. I am the smallest planet. **Pluto**

6. I am a beautiful planet because my wide rings are very wide. **Saturn**

7. We are the two planet neighbors of Earth (the closest planets to Earth). **Venus and Mars**

8. I am the third planet from the Sun. **Earth**

9. I am the number of planets in the solar system. **nine**

10. I am the number of satellites found around Neptune. **eight**

11. I am the seventh planet from the Sun. **Uranus**

12. I am usually the ninth planet. **Pluto**

13. I am the planet that has 3 rings and 16 satellites. **Jupiter**

14. I am the planet with the most satellites. **Saturn**

15. I give light and heat to all the planets. **Sun**

16. I am a body that orbits planets. **satellite or moon**

© 1996 Kelley Wingate Publications   37   KW 1601

Name _____
Skill: Celestial Bodies

What Is A Star?

Why is it that Miss Baker can only see stars at night? During the daytime stars twinkle and shine, but they are hard to see. That is because another star, our Sun, is shining brightly on the Earth. At night, we are turned away from our Sun and can see the other stars better. Our night sky is filled with small spots of light, most of which are stars from our galaxy and others beyond ours. Each of these little spots of light is actually a burning ball of gas and dust, just like our Sun. They give off heat and light. A few of the "stars" are not really stars at all. They are planets that reflect the Sun's light (like a mirror) and just look like they are shining.

Miss Baker needs help. She wants to break the code and find out what makes a star so bright. Help her decode the message below.

A B C D E F G H I J K L M N O P Q R S T U V W X Y Z
Z Y X W V U T S R Q P O N M L K J I H G F E D C B A

A STAR IS A BALL
Z HGZI RH Z YZOO

OF HYDROGEN,
LU SBWILTVM

HELIUM, AND DUST
SVORFN ZMW WFHG

THAT IS BURNING.
GSZG RH YFIMRMT

It gives off **HEAT** and **LIGHT.**
SVZG   ORTSG

© 1996 Kelley Wingate Publications   38   KW 1601

Name _____
Skill: Celestial Bodies

How Large Is A Star?

Miss Baker wants you to know that stars, like people, come in different sizes! Our Sun seems very large. It looks much larger than other stars because we are so close to it. The Sun also seems large because it is quite big. It would take over 100 Earths next to each other to fit across the center of the Sun! Although that size seems huge to us, our Sun is really only a medium (or middle) sized star! There are stars much smaller than the Sun. One small star named van Maanen's is about the same size as Mars. One of the largest stars is Betelgeuse. It is so enormous that our whole Solar System could fit inside it!

Use the information above to answer these questions.

1. Are all stars the same size as our Sun? **no**

2. Name a star that is smaller than our Sun: **van Maanen's**

3. Name a star that is larger than our Sun: **Betelgeuse**

4. How many Earths would fit across the center of the Sun? **100**

5. Is the Sun a small, medium, or large star? **medium**

6. Why does our Sun seem so huge to us? **It is much larger than Earth**

Using the information from above, label these three stars: Sun, van Maanen, and Betelgeuse.

Betelgeuse   **Sun**   **van Maanen's**

© 1996 Kelley Wingate Publications   39   KW 1601

Name _____
Skill: Celestial Bodies

What Is The North Star?

If you were to stand on the North Pole and look straight up, you would see Polaris (also called the North Star). As the Earth orbits the Sun, stars seem to "move" across the sky. The stars don't really move, we just see them from a different place in space. Polaris is the one star that is always in the same northern spot in our sky. For many years, sailors and hikers have used the North Star to help them figure out which direction they are traveling. The North Star shines brightly in our night sky, even though it is very far away from earth. It is so far away that it takes 782 years for the the light from the North Star to reach Earth!

Answer the following questions.

1. What is another name for the North Star? **Polaris**

2. Why do you think Polaris is called "the North Star"? **It is always above the North Pole**

3. How does the North Star help sailors and hikers? **They use it to figure out directions**

4. Why do the other stars seem to move during the year? **The Earth changes position as it orbits the Sun**

5. How long does it take for the light from the North Star to reach the Earth? **782 years**

© 1996 Kelley Wingate Publications   40   KW 1601

Answer Key

Name

Skill: Celestial Bodies

Our Sun Is A Star

The Earth is very close to a star. That star is called the Sun and is the center of our solar system. The Sun gives us the heat and light we need in order to live. The Sun is only a medium sized star, yet it would take one million Earths squeezed into a ball to equal the size of the Sun! The Sun is about five billion years old. Scientists believe that the Sun is half-way through its life and will burn for another five billion years or so. All of the energy of the Sun comes from gases that are burning in the core, or center. The energy is changed to heat and light as it reaches the surface of the Sun. The heat and light are radiated (given off) and travels through space to warm the Earth and give us light. On a hot summer day, the Sun may seem as if it is close enough to touch because it feels so hot. However, the Sun is really 150 million kilometers (93 million miles) away!

Use the information given above to answer these questions.

1. What two things does the Sun give us? *heat and light*

2. In what part of the sun is energy made? *the core*

3. How old is the Sun? *about 5 billion years old*

4. How far is the Earth from the Sun? *150 million km. 93 million mi.*

5. How many Earths would it take to equal the size of the Sun? *one million*

6. What happens to the Sun's energy as it reaches the surface of the Sun? *it changes to heat and light*

© 1996 Kelley Wingate Publications   41   KW 1601

Name

Skill: Celestial Bodies

Sunspots

A few hundred years ago, a scientist noticed black spots on the surface of the Sun. These dark spots are called sunspots, but no one really knows what causes them. We do know that sunspots are the coolest places on the surface of the Sun (but even these spots are still too hot to go near). Sunspots can last for as short as a few hours or as long as a year! Scientists have noticed that sunspots usually come in groups. These groups return to the same places on the Sun about every eleven years.

To learn the name of the scientist and the year in which he discovered sunspots, solve the code below.

The name of the scientist is ___ *GALILEO*
17 11 22 19 22 15 25

He discovered sunspots in the year ___ *1612*
AA FF AA BB

To see the sunspots, this scientist used a ___ *TELESCOPE*
30 15 22 15 29 13 25 26 15

When do sunspots return to the same place? *11 YEARS*
AA AA 35 15 11 28 29

11 = A	22 = L	33 = W
12 = B	23 = M	34 = X
13 = C	24 = N	35 = Y
14 = D	25 = O	36 = Z
15 = E	26 = P	AA = 1
16 = F	27 = Q	BB = 2
17 = G	28 = R	CC = 3
18 = H	29 = S	DD = 4
19 = I	30 = T	EE = 5
20 = J	31 = U	FF = 6
21 = K	32 = V	

Draw the Sun and a few sunspots:

© 1996 Kelley Wingate Publications   42   KW 1601

Name

Skill: Celestial Bodies

Solar Prominences

Miss Baker thinks that solar prominences are really neat to watch. Solar prominences are streams of fire that shoot up from the surface of the Sun, turn, and loop back down again. Most solar prominences take about an hour from the start to finish, but some can last as long as several months. Our Sun may have many of these prominences on its surface at any given time. They can suddenly burst out of the Sun without warning. A solar prominence can shoot into the air as high as 41,700 km (25,000 mi) above the Sun!

Answer the questions below.

1. What is a solar prominence? *a loop of fire from the Sun*

2. When can solar prominences happen? *any time*

3. How high can a solar prominence travel above the Sun? *41,700 km / 25,000 mi*

4. How long do solar prominences last? *1 hour to several months*

Draw a solar prominence on the Sun below.

© 1996 Kelley Wingate Publications   43   KW 1601

Name

Skill: Celestial Bodies

Solar Eclipses

Miss Baker couldn't believe her eyes! She was outside on a sunny day when the Sun disappeared! What Miss Baker was really seeing was a solar eclipse. A solar eclipse is when the moon comes between the Earth and the Sun, blocking out all its light. The shadow from the moon falls on the Earth and it becomes as dark as night in the middle of the day! The moon is not really as big as the Sun, but it looks like it is. That is because the Sun is so much farther away than the moon so they seem to be the same size when they are in the sky together. Sometimes the moon passes over part of the Sun. That is called a partial eclipse. When the moon covers the Sun completely, it is called a total eclipse. Although total eclipses are not rare, they can only be seen from the same spot on the Earth once every 400 years! (BE CAREFUL! NEVER look directly at the Sun, especially during a solar eclipse. The Sun's powerful rays could blind you.)

Below is a drawing of a solar eclipse. Label the Sun, Moon, and Earth then answer the questions.

Sun   MOON   EARTH

1. What is a solar eclipse? *When the moon blocks all or part of the Sun*

2. Why does the Earth become so dark? *The moon's shadow falls on the Earth*

3. Why must you never look directly at the Sun? *It could blind you*

© 1996 Kelley Wingate Publications   44   KW 1601

Answer Key

Star Struck (page 45)

Name _____ Skill: Celestial Bodies

Miss Baker noticed that the "star" words have became jumbled in space. Help her to unscramble these words.

- NNEMIROCPE — Prominence
- NSU — Sun
- PLISCEE — Eclipse
- LEETGEESUB — Betelgeuse
- ONOM — Moon
- RAHET — Earth
- LASOR — Solar
- TOPNUSS — Sunspot
- AHET — Heat
- GTILH — Light
- PARISOL — Polaris

© 1996 Kelley Wingate Publications   45   KW 1601

What Is A Constellation (page 46)

Name _____ Skill: Celestial Bodies

Have you ever tried to count all the stars in the sky? If you could do it, you would probably count about 2,000 stars. Early scientists wanted to study the stars, but it was difficult to keep track of so many. They noticed that some of the stars were grouped together and looked like a picture. By playing "connect the dots" with the stars, scientists were able to make 88 pictures that used every star in the sky! These star "pictures" of people, animals, and things are called constellations. Ursa Major and Ursa Minor are constellations that look like bears. The constellation Leo looks like a lion while Draco becomes a dragon. Seeing the stars as part of a picture made it easier to find the stars scientists wanted to watch each night. People enjoyed the idea of constellations and made up many stories about these "star pictures" that are still told today.

Use the information given above to answer these questions.

1. What is a constellation? Group of stars that make a picture
2. How did early scientists use constellations? used to locate position of stars
3. Name four constellations:
   Ursa Major   Ursa Minor   Leo   Draco
4. Connect the dots to see the constellation known as the "Big Dipper".

© 1996 Kelley Wingate Publications   46   KW 1601

WHAT IS A COMET? (page 47)

Name _____ Skill: Celestial Bodies

Have you ever made a snowball with dust and ice? Probably not, but that is how a comet is formed. Comets are very much like dirty snowballs that travel in a long, narrow orbit around the Sun. As they come closer to the Sun, some of the ice melts and makes a sort of cloud (called the coma) of gas and dust around the snowball. One strange fact about the comet is that its tail always points away from the Sun. As the comet comes toward the Sun, the tail is behind it. After the comet passes the Sun and is moving away, the tail is in front of it! Scientists think this might be caused by the strong solar winds from the Sun. These winds push the tail away, no matter which way the comet is headed.

Use the information above to answer these questions.

1. What is a comet? A dirty snowball that orbits the Sun
2. What makes a tail of a comet? ice melts as it nears the Sun and cloud is pushed away from Sun
3. What is unusual about the tail of a comet? It always points away from the Sun
4. What do scientists think pushes the tail of the comet away from the Sun?
5. Draw the tail of the comet below. (It is going toward the Sun.)

Sun

© 1996 Kelley Wingate Publications   47   KW 1601

HALLEY'S COMET (page 48)

Name _____ Skill: Celestial Bodies

What would you think if you saw a shiny ball with a long tail crossing the dark sky? That is what a comet looked like to people many years ago. They had no idea what comets really were. Maybe they thought a star had come loose and was flying through space! Comets are rare sights, and not many people have seen more than one in their entire life. In 1705, a scientist named Edmund Halley figured out how comets work. He studied a comet and realized that it was probably the same one the world had seen 76 years earlier. Halley gave us the idea that comets have orbits around the Sun, just like the planets. He predicted that his comet would return in 76 more years. Halley was right and his comet (since named Halley's Comet) returns to our part of space every 76 years!

Solve the following problems then crack the code to learn more about Halley's Comet.

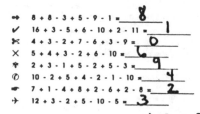

- 8 + 8 - 3 + 5 - 9 - 1 = 8
- 16 + 3 - 5 + 6 - 10 + 2 - 11 = 1
- 4 + 3 - 2 + 7 - 6 + 3 - 9 = 0
- 5 + 4 + 3 - 2 + 6 - 10 = 6
- 2 + 3 - 1 + 5 - 2 + 5 - 3 = 9
- 10 - 2 + 5 + 4 - 2 - 1 - 10 = 4
- 7 + 1 - 4 + 8 + 2 - 6 + 2 - 8 = 2
- 12 + 3 - 2 + 5 - 10 - 5 = 3

1. Halley's comet appeared in the year 1910 and was last seen in 1986.
2. It will return in 2062 and again in 2138.

© 1996 Kelley Wingate Publications   48   KW 1601

© 1996 Kelley Wingate Publications   118   CD-3727

Answer Key

Name _____ Skill: Celestial Bodies

ASTEROIDS

Asteroids are pieces of rock and metal that orbit a star. Scientists believe asteroids may be pieces of planets that were never formed. Most of the asteroids in our solar system orbit the Sun in a belt between Mars and Jupiter. This group is called the Asteroid Belt. The asteroids in this belt range in size from 1 km (0.6 mi) to about 1000 km (600 mi) wide. The largest asteroid in this belt has been named Ceres and is 1038 km (623 mi) wide! A much smaller belt known as the Trojan group is much further away from the Sun. Some asteroids, like the small one named Icarus, orbit by themselves along their own path.

Break the code to find out more about the largest asteroid in the Asteroid Belt.

A B C D E F G H I J K L M N O P Q R S T U V W X Y Z
Z Y X W V U T S R Q P O N M L K J I H G F E D C B A

The largest
G S V   O Z I T V H G

ASTEROID IS
Z H G V I L R W   R H

CERES. IT IS AS
X V I V H   R G   R H   Z H

LARGE AS THE
O Z I T V   Z H   G S V

STATE OF TEXAS.
H G Z G V   L U   G V C Z H

© 1996 Kelley Wingate Publications   49   KW 1601

Name _____ Skill: Celestial Bodies

METEORITES

We saw a flash of light in the sky last night. It looked like a star that was falling to the ground. Miss Baker explained that bits of rock, metal, and dust called meteoroids are floating around in space. The Earth's gravity pulls these meteoroids into the Earth's atmosphere and they begin to burn as they fall to the ground. As they are burning they are called meteors. Most of the time meteors burn up completely as they fall. Sometimes, however, meteors will reach the ground. Then they are called meteorites. The Earth is hit by many meteorites every year. Most of them are so small no one ever notices. Some are very large, but they most of these have fallen in places where few people live. One of the largest meteorites ever found is as large as a car. It is kept in a museum in New York.

Fill in the blanks.

1. A meteoroid is _a bit of rock or metal in space_

2. The Earth's _gravity_ pulls meteoroids into our atmosphere where they begin to burn.

3. A burning meteoroid is called a _meteor_

4. Most meteors burn up in the atmosphere. If they don't, they _fall to the ground_

5. Most meteors _burn up_ before they reach the ground.

6. When a meteor falls to the ground, it is then called a _meteorite_

7. The Earth is hit by _many_ meteorites every year, but most are never found.

8. One large meteorite can be found _in a museum in New York_

© 1996 Kelley Wingate Publications   50   KW 1601

Name _____ Skill: Celestial Bodies

A SHOWER WITHOUT WATER?

Have you ever taken a shower without water? That would be hard to do, but there are showers without water. A meteor shower doesn't have any water. A meteor shower is when hundreds of meteors enter the Earth's atmosphere and fall burning through the sky like a shower of fire. These events happen every few years and are exciting to watch!

Use the code below to learn about a remarkable meteor shower that happened in 1966.

A B C D E F G H I J K L M N O P Q R S T U V W X Y Z
10 20 30 40 50 60 70 80 90 15 25 35 45 55 65 75 85 95 16 17 18 19 1 2 3 4

THE LEONID
17 80 50   35 50 65 55 90 40

METEOR SHOWER
45 50 17 50 65 95   16 80 65 1 50 95

HAD OVER ONE
80 10 40   65 19 50 95   65 55 50

THOUSAND
17 80 65 18 16 10 55 40

METEORS BURNING
45 50 17 50 65 95 16   20 18 95 55 90 55 70

EVERY SECOND.
50 19 50 95 3   16 50 30 65 55 40

© 1996 Kelley Wingate Publications   51   KW 1601

Name _____ Skill: Celestial Bodies

A MIXED UP METEOR SHOWER

Miss Baker looked up in the sky one night and saw this strange meteor shower. Help her to arrange the words in the meteors to form a sentence that tells about a special meteorite.

can 000
meteorite XXXX
seen +++
crater XX
In ++
A X
be 0000
by 0
made 00
Arizona +
a XXX

A crater made by
X   XX   00   0

a meteorite can be
XXX   XXXX   000   0000

seen in Arizona.
+++   ++   +

This crater is 4,134 feet wide and 558 feet deep!

© 1996 Kelley Wingate Publications   52   KW 1601

Page 53 — SCRAMBLED SENTENCES

Name _____ Skill: Celestial Bodies

SCRAMBLED SENTENCES

Miss Baker was bringing you a group of sentences from outer space. Her spacecraft was hit by a meteor shower and the sentences got mixed up. Please help her to unscramble them so they make sense again.

1. Comet seen in be 2062 Halley's will again.

Halley's Comet will be seen again in 2062.

2. large of or metal rock are pieces Asteroids.

Asteroids are large pieces of metal or rock.

3. the Texas asteroid of Is Ceres size An named.

An asteroid named Ceres is the size of Texas.

4. no in meteor There is shower water a.

There is no water in a meteor shower.

5. like dirty of ice ball a comet is A.

A comet is like a dirty ball of ice.

6. away faces from the comet tail The a Sun of always.

The tail of a comet always faces away from the Sun.

7. that make are groups stars Constellations pictures of.

Constellations are groups of stars that make pictures.

© 1996 Kelley Wingate Publications   53   KW 1601

Page 54 — A NEW WORLD

Name _____ Skill: Celestial Bodies

A NEW WORLD

You have learned a lot about our Solar System. Wouldn't it be fun to discover a new one? Pretend that Miss Baker has taken you to a brand new solar system that is far beyond our own. The star is about the same size as our Sun, but this solar system has only three planets. As you travelled through the new solar system, you took notes about the planets (listed below). Use your notes to draw a picture of this solar system so the world can see what it looks like. You need to give a name to the system, its planets, and the moons.

My notes on the new solar system:

1. A middle sized star is the center of the solar system. It is yellow, like our Sun.

2. The planet closest to the star is the smallest. It is blue and has three smaller moons. All of the moons are grey and about the same size.

4. The second planet is blue and green. It looks as if it has land and water like the Earth does! This planet is larger than the first, but smaller than the third. It has two purple moons.

5. The third planet is the largest of the three. It is yellow and looks as if it may be made of gas. This planet also has three rings that circle it. The outer ring is orange, the middle ring is purple, and the inner ring is blue. This planet has no moons.

6. Name this new solar system: *answers will vary*

7. Name the star: _____

8. Name each of the planets: _____
_____
_____

9. Name the five moons: _____
_____
_____
_____
_____

© 1996 Kelley Wingate Publications   54   KW 1601

Page 55 — STAR WORDSEARCH

Name _____ Skill: Celestial Bodies

STAR WORDSEARCH

Finds these words in the puzzle above. (They may go backwards!)

ASTEROID	HALLEY	PROMINENCE
BETELGEUSE	METEOR	SOLAR
CERES	METEORITE	STAR
COMET	METEOROID	SUNSPOT
ECLIPSE	POLARIS	

© 1996 Kelley Wingate Publications   55   KW 1601

Page 56 — STAR CROSSWORD

Name _____ Skill: Celestial Bodies

STAR CROSSWORD

ACROSS

1. A lot of meteors falling at once.
5. When the Sun gets blocked by the moon
9. A meteor that reaches the ground
10. A "dirty snowball" that orbits the Sun

DOWN

2. This man has a comet named after him
3. A dark spot on the Sun
4. Bits of rock or metal floating in space
6. A flame that loops from the Sun
7. Large pieces of rock or metal that orbit the Sun
8. A ball of burning gas that gives off heat and light

© 1996 Kelley Wingate Publications   56   KW 1601

Name _____ Skill: Celestial Bodies

HUBBLE TELESCOPE

A telescope is an instrument that looks out into space and makes the planets, stars, and moons seem larger and closer to us than they really are. The Hubble telescope, which is named after Edwin Hubble, is the largest telescope of its kind. This telescope can see more stars than any telescope on earth. Why? It is not on the Earth, but is flying about 404 miles above the Earth as a satellite! The Hubble telescope is almost as large as a school bus with a mirror that is 8 feet across. The mirror acts as an "eye" for the telescope. There are also two cameras and special detectors that can see even the smallest source of light. It could see something as small as a flashlight on the Moon. The Hubble telescope satellite was built to last for years. When a problem arises that needs to be fixed, a space shuttle can be sent up to fix it!

Answer the following questions.

1. What is the Hubble telescope? *a huge telescope on a satellite*

2. Who was the telescope named for? *Edwin Hubble*

3. Why can the Hubble telescope see better than a telescope on Earth? *It is closer to the planets*

4. How many cameras does the Hubble telescope have? *2 cameras*

5. How big is the mirror on this telescope? *8 feet across*

6. How can this telescope be fixed if it breaks? *a space shuttle can be sent to fix it*

© 1996 Kelley Wingate Publications   57   KW 1601

Name _____ Skill: Space Exploration

ROCKETS AWAY!

Miss Baker was playing in the yard one day. She threw a ball up into the air. Almost right away, the ball fell back to Earth. Miss Baker knew that this was due to gravity, the force which holds us to Earth. How, then, can we launch rockets into space? Shouldn't they just fall right back to the Earth?

Actually, in order for a rocket to fly into space, it must break the force of gravity. How can it do this? The answer is a speed of 40,000 kilometers per hour. If you could throw a ball this fast, it would go up in the sky and never return!

Follow Miss Baker in her rocket. Pick up the letter on each planet to form a sentence about space.

ONE OF AMERICA'S FIRST MANNED ROCKETS WAS MERCURY.

© 1996 Kelley Wingate Publications   58   KW 1601

Name _____ Skill: Space Exploration

ROCKET MATH

Subtract the math problems below to find out about the first rockets.

23	15	39	24	18	50	16	40	79
-13	-7	-25	-7	-9	-34	-7	-29	-67
10	8	14	17	9	16	9	11	12

41	62	25	67	36	49	20	39	54
-28	-39	-8	-48	-18	-25	-9	-27	-34
13	23	17	19	18	24	11	12	20

58	44	25	30	31	91	59
-38	-26	-15	-15	-19	-69	-38
20	18	10	15	12	22	21

8	9	10	11	12	13	14	15	16	17	18	19	20	21	22	23	24
H	A	C	D	E	G	I	K	M	N	O	P	R	S	T	U	W

C H I N A   M A D E

G U N P O W D E R

R O C K E T S .

© 1996 Kelley Wingate Publications   59   KW 1601

Name _____ Skill: Space Exploration

WHAT MAKES A ROCKET FLY?

What makes a rocket move fast enough to break away from gravity? It needs energy, and lots of it. A car uses gas, or fuel, to give it energy. Your body uses food to make energy. A rocket needs fuel, too. The fuel tanks on a rocket hold liquid oxygen and hydrogen. When these two gases are mixed and burned, the fire and heat (energy) escapes from the bottom of the rocket. The energy that is made is strong enough to push the rocket away from the Earth. It goes right up through the atmosphere and into space! The gravity in space is not strong at all. Once the rocket is outside our atmosphere, it takes less fuel and energy to push the rocket where ever it is going.

Answer the questions below.

1. What is made from fuel? *energy*

2. What type of fuel does a car use? *gas*

3. What fuel does your body use? *food*

4. Name the two fuels used by rockets: *liquid oxygen and hydrogen*

5. What must be done with the two rocket fuels in order to make energy? *they must be mixed and burned*

6. How does this large amount of energy help move a rocket? *It is strong enough to push the rocket away from the Earth.*

7. Why does it take less energy to move a rocket once it is in space? *There is less gravity in space*

© 1996 Kelley Wingate Publications   60   KW 1601

Answer Key

Name _____ Skill: Space Exploration

SPACE AGE BEGINS

In 1883, a Russian schoolteacher wrote a paper that explained how rockets could be made that would travel to space. For the next 25 years scientists tried to make such a rocket. In 1926 the first rocket was successfully launched. It only went 41 feet in the air (not even close to space). The importance of this rocket was in showing scientists that rockets really could fly. After that, several countries began a race for space. On October 4, 1957, the Soviet Union launched the first rocket to orbit the Earth. The name of the rocket was Sputnik. The space age had finally begun!

Circle every fourth letter and write it on the blanks below to discover the American who launched that first rocket.

W T (R) G P L (O) B N M (B) W S A (E) Q

U I (R) X C (T) G I L (G) P Q Z (O) S Y

U (D) C W I (D) F D S (A) G H O (R) V R T

(D) V Z

The scientist's name : **ROBERT GODDARD**

Now unscramble some of the words in the following sentence to discover more about his experiment.

This <u>kcero t</u>   **rocket**   was launched with

liquid <u>lleu</u>   **fuel**   . It only went up about

41 <u>etef</u>   **feet**   into the in air. That was

enough to <u>vopre</u>   **prove**   that rockets really could fly.

© 1996 Kelley Wingate Publications   61   KW 1601

Name _____ Skill: Space Exploration

WHAT ARE ROCKET STAGES?

Rockets are spacecraft that are made up of stages (sections). Most of the rockets used for space travel have three stages. The first stage is full of fuel that is burned quickly during lift-off. This stage is jettisoned (dropped) as the rocket reaches the thin atmosphere near space. The second stage is also filled with fuel. This stage continues to push the rocket away from the Earth and is jettisoned when all the fuel has been burned. Stage two burns up as it drops back to the Earth. The third stage carries the payload (a satellite or a space capsule) into space and, finally, back to Earth. A capsule is a spacecraft where astronauts or cosmonauts sit. The first capsules had only one seat and were quite small. They were full of computers and equipment needed to control the spacecraft. Later capsules were larger and had room for three travelers.

Answer the following questions.

1. What is another name for the stage of a rocket?
   Section

2. How many stages do most rockets have?
   three stages

3. What is the purpose of the first stage (what does it do)?
   It pushes the rocket away from Earth.

4. What is the purpose of the second stage?
   It pushes the rocket to the edge of space

5. What happens to the first and second stages after all the fuel has been burned?
   They are jettisoned or dropped

6. What does the third stage carry?
   the payload (a satellite or capsule)

7. How are newer capsules different from the first ones that were used?
   They are larger and have 3 seats.

© 1996 Kelley Wingate Publications   62   KW 1601

Name _____ Skill: Space Exploration

THE FIRST SPACECRAFT

Miss Baker remembers hearing about the Soviet Union sending the first satellite into space in 1957. It was a metal ball that had a transmitter and batteries so that it could send signals back to Earth. The satellite circled the Earth for three weeks until the batteries ran down and could not send any more signals. Beep! Beep!

These signals were sent back to Earth. To solve the code, start at the arrow. Write the first letter (S) on the first blank below. Count three letters to the right (P). Put that letter on the second blank. Continue to write every third letter in order on the blanks below. The last letter (X) will not be used.

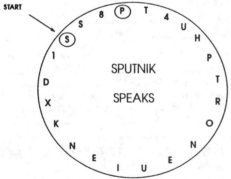

START

SPUTNIK

SPEAKS

The first satellite was **S P U T N I K** . It weighed **1 8 4 P O U N D S** and circled the Earth for **T H R E E** weeks.

© 1996 Kelley Wingate Publications   63   KW 1601

Name _____ Skill: Space Exploration

FIRST ANIMALS IN SPACE

Miss Baker was not the first animal in space. On November 3, 1957 a dog was launched into space by the Soviet Union. The dog flew in Sputnik 2 and circled the Earth for a week. Special equipment was attached to her body to let scientists know how she was reacting to her new home.

To learn more about animals in space, solve the code.

11 12 13 14 15 16 17 18 19 20 21 22 23 24 25 26 27 28 29 30 31 32 33 34 35 36
Z Y X W V U T S R Q P O N M L K J I H G F E D C B A

The first dog in space was named **L A I K A**
25 36 28 26 36

Other **A N I M A L S** that **F L E W**
36 23 28 24 36 25 18   31 25 32 14

In **R O C K E T S** included **M I C E**
19 22 34 26 32 17 18   24 28 34 32

and **G U I N E A   P I G S**
30 16 28 23 32 36   21 28 30 18

1. On what date was the first dog launched into space?
   November 3, 1957

2. What was the name of the rocket she flew in?
   Sputnik 2

3. How long did the dog stay in space?
   one week

4. Why do you think animals were used in rocket travel before men?
   They didn't know what would happen.

© 1996 Kelley Wingate Publications   64   KW 1601

© 1996 Kelley Wingate Publications   122   CD-3727

Answer Key

SPACE GARBAGE

Where do you throw your garbage? You probably throw it in a trash bag that will be recycled or buried in a landfill. Trash that is left in space cannot be recycled or buried. What trash is left in space? Old satellites, parts of rockets, nuts, bolts, empty fuel tanks, and paint that has chipped off a spacecraft are some things that have become "space trash". Space is so huge that a little trash might not seem like much of a problem, but it can be. Our "space trash" will not decompose (rot away) like much of our garbage on Earth does. This trash will stay in space and orbit a planet or the Sun. Future spacecraft may run into this trash! It might crash into a planet if it comes close enough to be pulled in by the gravity.

Rearrange these words to make sentences about space trash. Answer the last question.

1. leave trash pieces in space Spacecraft of may.
   Spacecraft may leave pieces of trash in space.

2. decompose space in Trash trash will not.
   Trash will not decompose in space.

3. run Spacecraft may trash into.
   Spacecraft may run into trash.

4. planet crash a into may trash Space.
   Space trash may crash into a planet.

5. dangerous trash Space a problem is.
   Space trash is a dangerous problem.

6. What do you think we could do to clean up the trash in space?
   (answers will vary)

© 1996 Kelley Wingate Publications   69   KW 1601

MAN ON THE MOON

Miss Baker was very excited on July 16, 1969. That day became a part of history as man stepped on the surface of the Moon for the very first time! The Apollo 11 spacecraft orbited the Moon as its lunar module (LM) called the Eagle landed in a basin called the Sea of Tranquility. Cameras sent pictures back to the Earth so the world could watch this event on their televisions. A few hours after landing, Neil Armstrong became the first man to walk on the Moon. Neil Armstrong and Edwin Aldrin collected samples of Moon rocks a dust to bring back to the Earth.

Solve the code to see what Neil Armstrong said as he stepped from the Eagle to the moon.

1	2	3	4	5	6	7	8	9	10	11	12	13	14	15	16
A	D	E	F	G	H	I	K	L	M	N	O	P	R	S	T

"THAT'S ONE SMALL
STEP FOR MAN.
ONE GIANT LEAP
FOR MANKIND."

© 1996 Kelley Wingate Publications   70   KW 1601

THE SPACE SHUTTLE

Miss Baker took us to see a very different spacecraft. It takes off like a rocket, orbits the Earth like a satellite, and comes back to Earth like an airplane. It is the space shuttle and it is the first spacecraft that can be used over and over. The space shuttle has four main parts: the orbiter, the two solid rocket boosters, the huge external fuel tank, and a set of three main engines at the bottom of the orbiter.

The two solid rocket boosters and the three main engines give the shuttle enough power to lift off the launch pad. The shuttle moves up through the atmosphere toward space. About two minutes after lift-off, the two boosters drop off and parachute back to Earth. They land in the ocean where they will be picked up by a ship. About six minutes later, the fuel in the external tank has been completely used. The external tank is also dropped into the ocean. The main engines are then used push the shuttle into orbit around the Earth. For the next few days the shuttle will orbit the Earth while the astronauts conduct experiments. When the astronauts are ready to return to Earth, the engines push the shuttle back into the Earth's atmosphere. Now the shuttle is flown much like an airplane as it lands on a runway.

Answer the following questions.

1. Name the four parts of the space shuttle:
   orbiter
   two solid rocket boosters
   external fuel tank
   three main engines

2. What makes the space shuttle different from other spacecraft?
   It can be reused

3. What happens to the two solid rocket boosters and the external fuel tank?
   They are dropped into the ocean.

4. Which part of the shuttle pushes it into orbit and back into the atmosphere?
   The main engines

© 1996 Kelley Wingate Publications   71   KW 1601

MORE ABOUT THE SHUTTLE

Miss Baker took a tour of the space shuttle. She told us that this spacecraft can hold up to ten people (usually four astronauts and six other passengers). The shuttle has a flight deck where the pilot sits to guide the craft. There is a crew cabin where the people eat and sleep. Behind the cabin is a large cargo bay that can carry up to 29,300 kg (65,000) pounds of equipment (payload). Sometimes a laboratory is put in the cargo bay. That is where the scientists perform many experiments. Trips on the space shuttle can last for two days to over two weeks.

Unscramble these sentences to learn more about the space shuttle.

1. is launched from The shuttle space Kennedy Space Center.
   The space shuttle is launched from Kennedy Space Center.

2. be 50 times can The space used shuttle between 100 and.
   The space shuttle can be used between 50 and 100 times.

3. shuttle when in The orbit upside down it space flies is.
   The space shuttle flies upside down when it is in orbit.

4. called The is Spacelab laboratory.
   The laboratory is called Spacelab.

5. experiments do Mission lab specialists in the.
   Mission specialists do experiments in the lab.

© 1996 Kelley Wingate Publications   72   KW 1601

Name _____   Skill: Space Exploration

MY VERY OWN

Miss Baker has invited us on a trip in the space shuttle. We will be gone for about two weeks. The shuttle has all the food, clothing, and bedding we will need for our trip, but you might want to bring along a few personal things. Perhaps you would like to have a favorite toy, family picture, or some things to experiment with in space. Miss Baker said there isn't a lot of extra room on the shuttle, so all your items must fit inside one small shoebox. The box should not weigh more than two pounds (4.5 kg).

Pack a small shoebox with the items you would like to take on this trip. When you are finished packing, compare your items with a buddy then answer the questions below.

1. What items did you bring?

    answers will vary

2. Choose two of your items and tell why you brought them.

    answers will vary

3. Did you and your buddy choose any items that were alike? If so, list them.

    answers will vary

Name _____   Skill: Space Exploration

LIFT OFF!

Miss Baker has asked us to take a trip on the space shuttle. First, we are strapped into our seats for take-off. The countdown begins: 10...9...8...7...6...5...4...3...2...1... The two solid rocket boosters burn and push us upward. Lift-off takes place! After about two minutes the rocket boosters are used up and fall off the shuttle. Parachutes carry them down to the ocean so they can be picked up and reused another time. A few minutes later the fuel in the external tank is burned up. This tank is also dropped from the shuttle, but it cannot be reused. As it falls, it breaks into many pieces that fall into the ocean. Finally, the main engines push the orbiter into a path around the Earth. Now it is time to begin our space journey and start our experiments.

Solve the code to find the name of the first woman astronaut to ride the space shuttle.

15	19	23	28	31	35	38	45	49	55	59	63	69	73	78	82	89	99
P	Y	A	W	E	O	N	R	D	M	U	C	I	F	S	L	H	T

THE FIRST WOMAN
99 89 31   73 69 45 78 99   28 35 55 23 38

ASTRONAUT   to fly in the
23 78 99 45 35 38 23 59

SPACE SHUTTLE
78 15 23 63 31   78 89 59 99 99 82 31

WAS SALLY RIDE.
28 23 78   78 23 82 82 19   45 69 49 31

The first woman astronaut to fly in the Space Shuttle was:

    SALLY RIDE

Name _____   Skill: Space Exploration

INSIDE THE CABIN

Miss Baker will show us cabin of the space shuttle. The cabin has three floors (decks). The lower deck has storage containers for things we might need on our flight. The mid deck is a room where we will spend most of our time. This room has a tiny kitchen called a galley where we can prepare our food. It also has bunk beds, lockers, and a restroom. From here we can climb a ladder to the top deck which is called the flight deck. This is where the commander and pilot sit to guide the shuttle. The flight deck is filled with instruments and controls. It also has a number of windows so we can see what is in front, next to, and above the shuttle!

Answer the questions below.

1. How many levels are in the cabin? _3 levels_
   Name them:
   lower deck
   mid deck
   flight deck

2. What do you call the two crew officers that guide the space shuttle?
   The commander and pilot

2. What is the name used for the kitchen on the space shuttle?
   Galley

3. What will you find below the mid deck?
   lower deck with storage containers

4. How do you get to the flight deck from the mid deck?
   climb a ladder

5. To which level would you go to get the best view of Earth?
   flight deck

6. On what level is the restroom found?
   mid deck

Name _____   Skill: Space Exploration

I'M FLOATING!

After getting into orbit on the Space Shuttle, the first thing we notice is that Miss Baker is floating! So are we! There isn't enough gravity to hold us to the floor. We thought there was no gravity in space. Miss Baker told us that there is a tiny bit of gravity pulling on us, but it is so weak that it seems like there is none. This is called microgravity. Microgravity has some other affects on us as well. The blood in the lower part of our bodies now moves upward. We had to tighten our belts and shoelaces because our waists and feet are actually smaller in space! We are taller now, too. That is because there isn't as much gravity pulling against our backbones so they spread out a bit. Microgravity is a lot of fun!

To find out what else happens to your body in microgravity, unscramble the words below to make sentences.

1. feels a cold It getting like are you.
   It feels like you are getting a cold.

2. look eyes Your smaller.
   Your eyes look smaller.

3. dizzy and feel may You weak.
   You may feel dizzy and weak.

4. because muscles heart don't as work Your they hard weaken.
   Your heart muscles weaken because they don't work as hard.

5. disappear face on Wrinkles your.
   Wrinkles on your face disappear.

Skill: Space Exploration

INDOOR CLOTHES

The first astronauts had to wear heavy spacesuits while they were orbiting the Earth. In the space shuttle we get to wear comfortable cotton pants and tops. It is very much like being on an airplane! The main difference is that our clothes have special pockets that close so that we can keep many items in them. If we don't put items in our pockets or attach them to the walls, they will float all over the cabin. We could get hit by a flying object!

To find the names of the items Miss Baker keeps in her pockets, unscramble the letters on each line. Use the clues to help you unscramble the letters.

1. Clue: I am full of ink and I help you write.
   P N E
   PEN

2. Clue: I am filled with lead and I help you write.
   C L P N E I
   PENCIL

3. Clue: I am a place where you keep important notes.
   A A D T   K O B O
   DATA BOOK

4. Clue: You might wear me when we the Sun shines in the windows.
   N G S S S L U A E S
   SUN GLASSES

5. Clue: You might use me because you have the sniffles.
   S I T U S E
   TISSUE

6. Clue: You use me when you need to cut something.
   C I S O S R S S
   SCISSORS

77 KW 1601

Skill: Space Exploration

OUTDOOR CLOTHES

Miss Baker wants us to take a spacewalk outside. Before we can go, we must change into our spacesuit. Astronauts call this white suit an EMU (extravehicular mobility unit). Our EMU has three parts. The first part is the liner which looks like a pair of long johns. The liner has plastic tubes all through it to keep us cool or warm. Next comes our pressure vessel suit which includes our helmet and gloves. Finally, we put on our PLSS (primary life-supporting system). This looks like a backpack and has enough oxygen for seven hours! Ready?

Answer the questions below.

1. What must we wear to take a spacewalk?
   An EMU

2. What do the letters E.M.U. stand for?
   Extravehicular mobility unit

3. What do the letters P.L.S.S. stand for?
   Primary life-support system

4. What are the three parts of the spacesuit?
   liner
   pressure vessel suit
   PLSS

5. What does the liner do?
   Keeps us cool or warm

6. Which part of the spacesuit has the helmet and gloves?
   The pressure vessel suit

7. Why is the backpack filled with oxygen?
   So we can breathe in space

78 KW 1601

Skill: Space Exploration

LET'S GO!

Oh, dear! A part of the space shuttle needs to be repaired outside. You volunteer to go fix it. Miss Baker shows you into the airlock tunnel and closes the door. The door will keep oxygen in the cabin while you open the hatch to step into space. In the airlock, you change into your EMU spacesuit. You will have to move around the outside of the spacecraft so you reach for your MMU (manned maneuvering unit). When you strap it on, the MMU allows you to fly without being attached to the space shuttle. Now you unlock the hatch to the outside. Wow! You're floating with the stars!

Solve the code to see what you will find inside your space helmet.

```
A B C D E F G L O P Q R S T U V W X Z
N O P Q R S T U M W C I H F L D E B A
```

A WATER TUBE, FOOD, MICROPHONE, EARPHONES, AND A Q-TIP ARE FOUND IN THE HELMET.

79 KW 1601

Skill: Space Exploration

EATING IN SPACE

It is your turn to fix dinner tonight on board the Space Shuttle. Miss Baker will show you where the galley (kitchen) is in the cabin. There you will find a pantry (to store food), oven, hot and cold water, and trays. Sorry, there is no refrigerator on board the shuttle! There are over 100 foods and 20 drinks to choose from. You really don't need to know how to cook. The food has been prepared and packaged to make it easier to fix. You will only need to heat the food or add water as directed on each package. Dinner should be ready in about 30 minutes!

Some of the foods you will find on board the Shuttle are listed below. Plan a meal (breakfast, lunch, dinner, or snack) for your crew. Draw your meal on the plate below. Label each item.

Broccoli au gratin   Mixed vegetables   Green beans   Asparagus   Tomatoes

Applesauce   Bananas   Pears   Pudding

Dried apricots   Dried peaches

Pecan cookies   Graham crackers

orange drink   Peanuts

punch   coffee

Tea   Cocoa

Ham   Bread

Turkey   Jam and Jelly

Tuna fish   Peanut butter

Beef and gravy   BBQ Beef slices

Chicken a la king   Chicken and rice

Macaroni and cheese   Shrimp creole

Scrambled eggs   Cornflakes   Instant breakfast (Chocolate or strawberry)

answers will vary

Why do you think milk and butter are not part of the list? _____

80 KW 1601

Answer Key

Name _____   Skill: Space Exploration

SUPPER'S ON!

Guess what? Miss Baker tells us that we don't have to sit down for supper! We can stand up, hang from the ceiling, or push ourselves into a corner. The only rule is that we must be careful when we eat. Remember, food floats too! We must avoid spills so that the food will not litter the cabin. Floating food may get into some of the equipment and ruin it. Food that is left to float around begins to spoil and cause germs that may make us all sick. We have a special tray and a tiny spoon that helps us keep our food where it should be. Miss Baker says that the small spoon grabs the food better. Some of our food can be eaten right from the pouch it is packaged in. Eating in space is fun!

Oh, no! Miss Baker spilled her water, cookies, popcorn, and peas. Grab the pieces and unscramble them to make words that will complete the sentences below.

1. P L S I O	2. O O P S N
3. A O T L F	4. C R U L F A E

1. Floating food may __SPOIL__ and cause germs.

2. Miss Baker uses a small __SPOON__ for eating.

3. Anything not tied or held down will __FLOAT__ .

4. When eating in space, we must be very __CAREFUL__ .

© 1996 Kelley Wingate Publications   81   KW 1601

Name _____   Skill: Space Exploration

SPACELAB

Would you like to do any schoolwork in space? Miss Baker says that we can easily do science experiments during our flight. There is a big laboratory called Spacelab in the cargo bay. Ten countries worked together to build this flying laboratory so that experiments could be tested in space. In the lab we'll be able to grow crystals, test animals, look through special telescopes, and even take pictures of Earth. What do you want to do first?

To learn more about Spacelab, unscramble the words below to make sentences.

1. a in shuttle Spacelab is laboratory the.
Space lab is a laboratory in the shuttle.

2. is in cargo Spacelab kept the bay.
Spacelab is kept in the cargo bay.

3. countries Ten build helped Spacelab.
Ten countries helped build Spacelab.

4. experiments Scientists in do lab the.
Scientists do experiments in the lab.

5. in telescopes are special There Spacelab.
There are special telescopes in Spacelab.

6. can crystals We in grow space.
We can grow crystals in space.

7. have studied Spacelab and Scientists webs spiders in the.
Scientists have studied spiders and webs in the space lab.

8. pictures can take cameras of Special the Earth.
Special cameras can take pictures of the Earth.

© 1996 Kelley Wingate Publications   82   KW 1601

Name _____   Skill: Space Exploration

KEEPING FIT

Miss Baker told us that microgravity makes it easy to move in space. Our muscles do not have to work as hard when we are aboard the shuttle. After Miss Baker's last trip into space her muscles were weak and it was hard to get used to the gravity back on Earth. Scientists have learned that it is very important for the space travelers to exercise every day so that their muscles will stay strong. There is a treadmill on board that works your muscles as if you are walking on Earth. This machine even slants upward so that you can feel like you are climbing a hill! You can work up a real sweat on this machine! In microgravity, the droplets will not run off your face like they do on Earth. When you get on the treadmill you must turn on a special vacuum air cleaner that will pull the water away from your skin. This way you can keep fit without getting soaked!

Answer the questions below.

1. Why is it easier to move your body in space than on Earth?
less gravity pulls on you

2. Why is it important that astronauts exercise while traveling in space?
Exercise keeps the muscles strong.

3. What piece of exercise equipment is on the Space Shuttle?
a tread mill

4. Why does the treadmill slant?
It makes you "walk uphill".

5. Why must you turn on an air cleaner before exercising?
It pulls the sweat from your body.

6. What other exercises do you think astronauts might do to keep their muscles in shape?
Answers will vary.

© 1996 Kelley Wingate Publications   83   KW 1601

Name _____   Skill: Space Exploration

KEEPING CLEAN

At home you may take out the trash as a chore. In space, nothing can be thrown out because it would litter space. What will we do with our trash during our trip through space? All trash is sealed in plastic bags and put into a special storage container. We must be careful to clean the cabin every day so that germs will not spread and make us ill. We cannot take a shower or bath in space, but Miss Baker makes us wash our bodies with a wet cloth. After our wash, we will put on a clean shirt every three days and fresh pants once a week. Our dirty clothes are sealed in bags and stored in the same way as the trash. Don't forget to wipe off the food trays with a wet wipe after each meal. This keeps the trays clean and free of germs. There's a lot to keep clean in space!

Use the code to find the name of the trash or garbage sealed in each bag.

A C D E F H I L M N O P R S T U W

SHIRT   PANTS   WET WIPES

WASH CLOTH   FOOD   TISSUE

© 1996 Kelley Wingate Publications   84   KW 1601

© 1996 Kelley Wingate Publications   127   CD-3727

Answer Key

Name _____ Skill: Space Exploration

A MECHANICAL ARM

Miss Baker tells us that there is a satellite in the cargo bay. We need to get it moved outside the shuttle so it can orbit the Earth. The satellite is very heavy. We know we won't be able to lift it by ourselves. What can we do? Our problem is solved when Miss Baker explains that the space shuttle has a RMS (remote manipulator system). The RMS is a mechanical "arm" with joints just like a real arm! It is able to lift and move things that weigh much more than a man or woman can lift. The controls for the RMS are on the flight deck. First one to the flight deck gets to move the satellite!

Break the code to find out how to operate the RMS.

1	2	3	4	5	6	7	8	9	10	11	12	13	14	15	16	17	18
A	C	D	E	F	G	H	I	L	K	M	N	O	P	R	S	T	U

T H E   C O N T R O L   F O R
17 7 4   2 13 12 17 15 13 9   5 13 15

T H E   R M S   I S   A
17 7 4   15 11 16 8 16 1

C O M P U T E R   O N   T H E
2 13 11 14 18 17 4 15   13 12   17 7 4

F L I G H T   D E C K .
5 9 8 6 7 17   3 4 2 10

© 1996 Kelley Wingate Publications   85   KW 1601

Name _____ Skill: Space Exploration

FEELING ILL?

Sometimes astronauts on board the space shuttle may need some medical attention. They may cut themselves or feel a little ill. The astronauts keep a SOMS (Shuttle Orbiter Medical System) on board. This is like a first-aid kit with a few extra items. The SOMS has a stethoscope (to listen to the heart), a blood pressure cuff, sutures to use as stitches, thermometers, bandages, tape, and medicines. The astronauts hope they will not need to use the SOMS, but they are glad to take it along just in case!

Read each statement. Decide which item from the SOMS kit you would use. .

1. Randy was opening a food pouch to have a quick snack. He was going to use his pocket knife to open the pouch. Just as Randy opened the knife, the shuttle was hit by a small meteoroid. The shuttle is fine, but Randy cut himself on the arm. The cut is not large, but it is deep and is bleeding a lot. Randy needs the SOMS kit. He would probably use the

sutures (stitches)

2. Sally has not gotten used to the microgravity yet. She feels a little sick to her stomach. She will get the SOMS kit and will take some

medicine

3. Jamal's face looks red and he is sweating. He says he feels very hot. Jamal will need to take his temperature with a

thermometer

4. Kathy has just gotten off the treadmill. She may have overdone the exercise. She feels as though her heart is beating too fast. We can listen to her heartbeat with a

stethoscope

What do the letters "SOMS" stand for?

Shuttle Orbiter Medical System

© 1996 Kelley Wingate Publications   86   KW 1601

Name _____ Skill: Space Exploration

TIME FOR BED

It is been such a busy day that all of us are tired. Miss Baker asks us where we would like to sleep. There are several compartments that have a bunk bed. Each bunk has a mattress and pillow. There is also a reading light on the wall of each compartment. The bunk beds are comfortable, but it might be more fun to sleep on the floor or ceiling. Just be sure to attach the sleeping bag to something or you will float around the cabin as you sleep! Miss Baker tells us that getting enough sleep is just as important in space as it is on Earth. Remember to zip your arms inside the bag or strap them down. If you don't, you may wake up with your arms floating out in front of you!

Answer the following questions.

1. Name three items that are built into the bunk bed compartments.

mattress
pillow
reading light

2. If you don't care to sleep in a bunk bed, where else might you sleep?
on the floor or ceiling

3. Why should you strap your arms down before you go to sleep?
Your arms will float.

Follow the steps in this long math problem to find out how often the Sun sets when you orbit the Earth in the shuttle.

1. Write down the numeral 99 ___ 99
2. Subtract 12 ___ 87
3. Subtract 5 ___ 82
4. Subtract 32 ___ 50
5. Add 15 ___ 65
6. Subtract 20 ___ 45

The sun sets every ___45___ minutes when you orbit the Earth.

© 1996 Kelley Wingate Publications   87   KW 1601

Name _____ Skill: Space Exploration

COMING HOME

The time has come for us to return to Earth. Miss Baker tells us that we must put everything we don't need into storage. Nothing can be left floating around the cabin. We need to bolt our seats to the floor and close the cargo bay doors. When everything is put away and fastened down, it is time to get into our antigravity suits. These suits help our bodies adjust as the gravitational pull becomes stronger. The shuttle is turned around so it will enter the Earth's atmosphere backwards. Heat proof tiles cover the shuttle so the friction and heat will not burn up the spacecraft as we come back into the atmosphere. Reentry is complete! The engines are slowed and the shuttle is turned back around. The shuttle is now flown like an airplane. We can see the runway straight ahead. We are home again!

Do you want to know how many heat proof tiles cover the space shuttle? Solve the math problems below. Use the answers to find the correct numbers and put the answers in the blanks at the bottom of the page.

467	723	668	543	795
- 135	- 471	+ 122	+ 261	- 494
332	252	790	804	301

1. Find the digit that is in the tens place in the first problem. Write that number in the ten thousands place below.

2. Find the digit that is in the thousands place in the second problem. Write that number in the thousands place below.

3. Find the digit that is in the ones place in the third problem. Write that number in the hundreds place below.

4. Find the digit that is in the tens place in the fourth problem. Write that number in the tens place below.

5. Find the digit that is in the tens place in the fifth problem. Write that number in the ones place below.

The Space Shuttle has __32,000__ heat tiles.

© 1996 Kelley Wingate Publications   88   KW 1601

Name _____   Skill: Space Exploration

SPACE STATIONS

This afternoon Miss Baker told us about space stations. They are like cities that orbit the Earth. Space stations allow astronauts to stay in orbit for long periods of time. The Soviet Union set up one space station called Mir. A cosmonaut spent over a year there! A robot spacecraft (no people on board) brings fresh supplies and the mail from Earth to the space station. Other spacecraft can visit space stations when they need supplies. They can pick up food, water, and clean clothes at the space station.

Find out how many days the cosmonaut spent in space. Solve the math problems below then decode the message.

1. 20 x 2 = **40**   + 1 = **41**
2. 30 x 2 = **60**   + 5 = **65**
3. 10 + 15 = **25**   + 5 = **30**
4. 108 + 100 = **208** + 100 = **308**
5. 40 + 40 = **80**   + 15 = **95**
6. 50 x 2 = **100**   + 3 = **103**
7. 44 + 40 = **84**   + 4 = **88**
8. 11 + 11 = **22**   + 11 = **33**
9. 30 + 40 = **70**   +13 = **83**
10. 50 + 40 = **90**   + 7 = **97**

1. Find the digit that is in the tens place in the first problem. Write that number in the hundreds place below.

2. Find the digit that is in the hundreds place in the fourth problem. Write that number in the tens place below.

3. Find the digit that is in the tens place in the tenth problem. Write that number in the ones place below.

The cosmonaut spent **4 3 9** days in space.

Name _____   Skill: Space Exploration

TALK LIKE AN ASTRONAUT

"Put on your EMU because NASA says we have EVA to do!" Astronauts use acronyms for many of the things they talk about. Acronyms are short words made from the first letters or syllables of two or more words that make up a phrase. For example, EMU stands for the longer phrase "extravehicular mobility unit". Below is a list of common acronyms that astronauts use and a description of what each means.

NASA	National Aeronautics and Space Administration (the name of the United States space program)
PLSS	Portable Life-Support System (a backpack filled with oxygen)
EMU	Extravehicular Mobility Unit (a spacesuit)
EVA	Extravehicular Activity (any work done outside cabin)
SOMS	Shuttle Orbiter Medical System (a medical kit)
STS	Space Transportation System (the shuttle, tank, and boosters)
KSC	Kennedy Space Center (a launch site in Florida)
SRB	Solid Rocket Booster (the first fuel stage of a shuttle)
IVA	Intravehicular Activity (any work done inside the cabin)
MCC	Mission Control Center (a place in Texas that watches and helps control all United States space flights)
WMC	Waste Management Compartment (the bathroom)

Can you talk like an astronaut? Choose five acronyms and write a sentence for each.

1. _____ sentences will vary _____
2. _____
   _____
3. _____
4. _____
5. _____

Name _____   Skill: Space Exploration

DESIGN A CREW PATCH

Every mission that is taken in space has a crew patch designed for it. The patch gives the date, the name of the mission, and the names of the crew members.

Design the crew patch for the mission you went on with Miss Baker. Design your patch on another piece of paper first. Copy it neatly into the circle below then color it. Share your patch with the class.

Designs will vary

Name _____   Skill: Space Exploration

SPACE EXPLORATION CROSSWORD

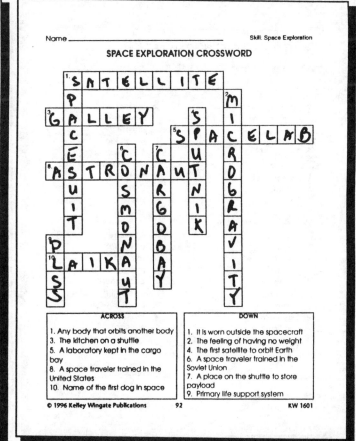

ACROSS
1. Any body that orbits another body
3. The kitchen on a shuttle
5. A laboratory kept in the cargo bay
8. A space traveler trained in the United States
10. Name of the first dog in space

DOWN
1. It is worn outside the spacecraft
2. The feeling of having no weight
4. The first satellite to orbit Earth
6. A space traveler trained in the Soviet Union
7. A place on the shuttle to store payload
9. Primary life support system

CD-3727

Answer Key

Page 93

Name _____   Skill: Space Exploration

SPACE EXPLORATION WORDSEARCH

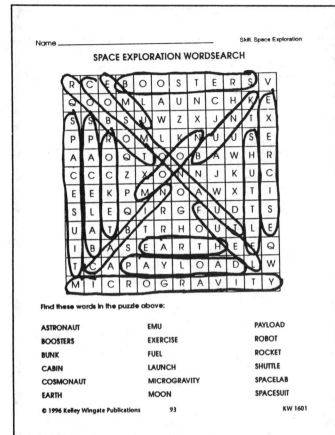

Find these words in the puzzle above:

ASTRONAUT	EMU	PAYLOAD
BOOSTERS	EXERCISE	ROBOT
BUNK	FUEL	ROCKET
CABIN	LAUNCH	SHUTTLE
COSMONAUT	MICROGRAVITY	SPACELAB
EARTH	MOON	SPACESUIT

© 1996 Kelley Wingate Publications   93   KW 1601

Page 94

Name _____   Skill: Space Exploration

SECRET MESSAGE

Add the problems and use the code to find out what the secret message is!

A	B	C	D	E	F	G	H	I	J	K	L	M
3	5	7	9	11	13	15	17	19	21	23	25	27

N	O	P	Q	R	S	T	U	V	W	X	Y	Z
2	4	6	8	10	12	14	16	18	20	22	24	26

T H E
7+7 8+9 6+5

S H U T T L E
6+6 10+7 9+7 6+8 12+2 12+13 4+7

C A N
4+3 1+2 1+1

B E
3+2 3+8

U S E D
8+8 5+7 2+9 3+6

T O
9+5 4+0

C A R R Y
6+1 2+1 5+5 7+3 12+12

C A R G O
2+5 0+3 2+8 13+2 1+3

T O
5+9 0+4

A N D
1+2 2+0 3+6

F R O M
7+6 9+1 3+1 17+10

S P A C E
10+2 5+1 2+1 4+3 2+9

© 1996 Kelley Wingate Publications   94   KW 1601

Page 95

Name _____   Skill: Space Exploration

SPACE WORD SYLLABLES

Write the number of syllables in front of each "space" word.

2	shuttle	3	Jupiter
3	orbiter	3	meteor
5	laboratory	1	Mars
3	satellite	2	crystal
2	runway	3	medicine
3	asteroid	2	Spacelab
2	comet	4	experiment
1	Earth	1	moon
2	planet	3	Uranus
3	telescope	1	stage
1	space	3	scientist
3	Mercury	2	Venus
2	Saturn	2	Neptune
2	Pluto	3	exercise
2	shuttle	2	mission
1	patch	5	microgravity
3	astronaut	3	cosmonaut
2	booster	4	constellation
1	flare	3	prominence
3	hydrogen	3	helium
2	eclipse	2	sunspot
1	star	2	Halley
1	dust	2	crater
1	rock	1	gas
2	solar	1	rings

© 1996 Kelley Wingate Publications   95   KW 1601

Page 96

Name _____   Skill: Space Exploration

E.T.

There is no known life on any of the other eight planets in our solar system. There are millions of stars like our Sun in our galaxy. Perhaps there is another planet orbiting one of those stars that has life! The word "extraterrestrial" (the acronym is E.T.) means any unknown form of life. What do you think an E.T. might look like? Scientists sometimes use Latin words to name plants or animals. For example, a "monocornis" would be a one horned animal. The name helps to describe the animal.

Draw a picture of the E.T. named in each example. Use the list of Latin words to help you. Create your own E.T. and give it the proper Latin name. You can draw it on the back of this paper.

WORD	MEANING
mono	one
bi	two
tri	three
quadro	four
pento	five
ped	foot (feet)
cornis	horn
cephalus	head
milano	black
lenco	white
erythro	red
bruno	brown
tencus	line
punctata	dotted

Any animal that has 4 legs, 2 heads, and spots or dots.

Punctata quadroped bicephalus

Any animal with black lines, red horns and 3 feet.

Milanolencus Erythrocornis Triped

© 1996 Kelley Wingate Publications   96   KW 1601

Answer Key

Name _____ Skill: Recall

HOW MUCH DO YOU REMEMBER?

Finish each statement or answer the question with a word or short answer.

1. Uranus was discovered in what year? **1781**
2. About how old is our Sun? **5 billion years old**
3. The planet closest to the Sun is **Mercury**
4. The EMU liner has **tubes** to help keep you cool.
5. Which planet has the most satellites? **Saturn**
6. An **eclipse** occurs when the Moon comes between the Sun and Earth.
7. What is the distance to the Sun from Earth? **93 million mi. 150 million km**
8. **Venus** is the planet closest to the Earth.
9. Which planet is known as Earth's sister planet? **Venus**
10. A **comet** is like a dirty ball of ice.
11. What comes near the Earth every 76 years? **Halley's comet**
12. **The North Star** is another name for Polaris.
13. What is the name of the largest star? **Betelgeuse**
14. How many stages do most rockets have? **3**
15. The smallest and coldest planet is **Pluto**
16. On what planet will you find the Great Red Spot? **Jupiter**
17. What is the name of Earth's satellite? **Moon**
18. A group of stars that make a picture is called a **constellation**

Name _____ Skill: Recall

19. About how many food items are carried on the Shuttle? **100**
20. About how many drink choices are carried on the Shuttle? **20**
21. **Microgravity** makes you feel weightless.
22. Our Sun is a **middle or medium** sized star.
23. A **star** gives off light and heat.
24. The planet **Earth** is the only known planet with life.
25. **Pluto** is the planet usually furthest from the Sun.
26. Triton is a moon of **Neptune**
27. The Caloris Basin can be found on **Mercury**
28. The **space shuttle** is a spacecraft that can be reused.
29. The planet **Venus** is also called the Evening Star.
30. The Great Dark Spot is found on the planet **Neptune**
31. A **cosmonaut** is a Soviet Union person trained for space travel.
32. **Mars** is also called "The Red Planet".
33. The Great Red Spot is a **storm** that is over 300 years old.
34. An **astronaut** is a United States person trained for space travel.
35. **Hydrogen** and **helium** are the two gases found in a star.
36. Over 100 **meteorites** fall to the ground on Earth each year.

Name _____ Skill: Recall

37. The first man to step on the Moon was **Neil Armstrong**
38. The fifth planet from the Sun is **Jupiter**
39. The planets are divided into inner and **outer planets**
40. **Uranus** has more rings than any other planet.
41. Name the four main parts of the Space Shuttle.
    1. **orbiter**
    2. **solid rocket boosters**
    3. **external fuel tank**
    4. **shuttle**
42. **Uranus** is a planet that is tipped on its side.
43. The Asteroid Belt orbits around the Sun between these two planets:
    1. **Mars**
    2. **Jupiter**
44. Dark spots on the Sun are called **sunspots**
45. When a meteor lands on Earth, it is called a **meteorite**
46. The kitchen on the space shuttle is called a **galley**
47. The first satellite to go into space was called **Sputnik**
48. Mir is a Russian **space station**
49. Valentina Tereshkova was the first **woman** in space.
50. In what year was the planet Neptune discovered? **1781**
51. A comet's tail always points **away from the Sun**
52. A solar **prominence** can loop as high as 25,000 miles from the surface of the Sun.

Name _____ Skill: Recall

53. Our solar system is in what galaxy? **the Milky Way**
54. Valles Marineris is found on what planet? **Mars**
55. **Uranus** is the seventh planet from the Sun.
56. Many heat proof **tiles** line the space shuttle to keep it from burning up as it reenters Earth's atmosphere.
57. Burning **fuel** makes enough energy to lift a rocket through the atmosphere into space.
58. There are **three** levels or decks on a shuttle.
59. What was the name of the first dog in space? **Laika**
60. Miss Baker was a **monkey** used in early space travel.
61. Which planet is between Jupiter and Uranus? **Saturn**
62. Venus is very hot during the day and very **cold** at night.
63. It takes **7x2** years for the light from the North Star to reach Earth.
64. **Galileo** was the scientist who used a telescope and discovered sunspots.
65. An eclipse happens when the **Moon** comes between the Sun and the Earth.
66. When the shuttle returns to Earth, it lands on a **runway**
67. How many people can the shuttle carry? **ten**
68. **Jupiter** is the largest planet.
69. The largest known asteroid is called **Ceres**

Name _____   Skill: Experiment

A CAREER IN SPACE

Would you like to grow up to be an astronaut? There are several things you can do to prepare for being an astronaut. You must:

1. Keep yourself in good physical condition. Exercise every day to make your muscles strong. Eat the proper foods to give your body energy.

2. Go to college. Graduate with a degree in engineering, science, or math.

3. Get an advanced degree (a masters or doctorate) or get a job in a space related field for at least three years.

Would you like to know more about becoming an astronaut or other jobs in the space program? Write a letter to one of the addresses below and ask for information.

Astronaut Selection Office
Education
NASA
Johnson Space Center
Houston, TX 77058

American Society for Aerospace
821 15th Street, N.W.
Washington, D.C. 20005

Civil Air Patrol
Attn: Aerospace Education and Cadet Training
National Headquarters
Maxwell AFB, AL 36112

It is best to write your ideas and questions on a practice page before you write the letter. List your questions here to help you organize your thoughts. When you are finished, a parent or teacher can help you address and mail the letter.

(Answers will vary)

Name _____   Skill: Experiment

MAKING A COMET

Miss Baker wants you to see what a comet looks like up close. Here is an experiment you can try with an adult.

Materials needed:
a large, open-mouthed pot
3 cups water
1 and 1/2 cups sand
a teaspoon of ammonia
rubber gloves
garbage bags
3 cups dry ice
a hammer or tool for pounding
a large metal spoon for stirring

1. Place garbage bag as a liner in the pot.

2. Put the water, sand, and ammonia into the pot and mix well.

3. ADULTS DO THIS! With rubber gloves on, wrap the dry ice inside several garbage bags.

4. With the hammer, smash the dry ice into small pieces.

5. Take 3 cups of this crushed dry ice and add to mixture in bowl.

6. Stir until almost frozen.

7. Lift the mixture inside the garbage bag from the pot.

8. With your gloved hands, shape the mixture into a ball.

9. Place the ball in a spot on the ground where everyone can see. DO NOT TOUCH!

10. As the dry ice changes into a gas, you will see trails of "smoke" coming from it. Pretend you are the solar wind and blow against the ball. Watch the tail form behind your "comet"!

Name _____   Skill: Experiment

MAKING YOUR OWN ROCKET

Would you like to see your own rocket travel through space? Try this experiment and you will see how rockets are pushed away from the Earth from the gas that escapes from the back of the rocket.

Materials needed:
12 feet (4 meters) of string
one large balloon
a clamp or clothespin
plastic drinking straw
masking tape.

1. Tie one end of the string to something heavy like a wooden chair or desk. This is your "launching pad".

2. Blow up the balloon. Clamp the stem of the balloon to hold in the air. The balloon will be your "rocket".

3. Cut the straw in half. Lay the two pieces end to end from the top of the balloon to the stem. Leave about an inch between the two pieces of straw. Use masking tape to attach the two sections of straw to the balloon. The straws will hold your "rocket" on course.

4. Start at the balloon stem and thread the loose end of the string through both sections of straw. Stretch the string out tightly and tie the end to another chair or heavy object. Make sure the string does not sag or touch the floor. The string will be the "orbit path" for your balloon.

5. Push the balloon back against the "launching pad". (Make sure that the balloon stem is facing the pad.) Now you are ready for lift-off.

6. Pull the clamp from the balloon stem! Zoom! The balloon will race to the other end of the string. Mission complete!

Tie another string along the same path and have race two balloons. See if the size of the balloon makes a difference in the speed at which it travels.

Name _____   Skill: Experiment

GROWING CRYSTALS

Astronauts have been experimenting with growing crystals in space. One thing they have found is that crystals can grow in space much faster than on Earth. A crystal is like a tiny brick that repeats itself in a pattern and grows. The "brick" comes in many different shapes like cubes, hexagons, or rectangles. Salt and sugar are common crystals that we use every day. Some gem stones such as quartz and amethyst are also crystals. You can grow your own crystals right here on Earth. They won't grow as fast as they do in space, so be patient!

Materials needed:
1 cup of very hot water
2 cups of sugar
1 pint jar
1 spoon
1 old towel
food coloring

1. Pour the hot water into the pint jar.

2. Mix in half a cup of sugar. Stir it with the spoon until all the sugar dissolves (disappears into the water). Keep adding half a cup of sugar at a time and stir until all of the sugar has been dissolved (both cups).

3. Would you like to make colored crystals? Add one or two drops of food coloring to make the crystals blue, red, green, or yellow.

4. Wrap the towel around the jar. The towel helps hold in the heat so the solution will cool slowly. Crystals will form only if the solution cools slowly. Keep the towel wrapped around the jar and be patient!

5. Set the jar in a place where it will not be bumped or disturbed. (Movement will stop the crystals from growing.)

6. Leave the jar alone for two to three days. Groups of sugar crystals will form on the top and bottom of the jar. A few may even form along the sides.

Keep up the Great Work!

_____ **earns this award for**

_____

You are TERRIFIC!

_____ _____

Signed   Date

Certificate of Completion

This certificate certifies that

_____

Has completed

_____

_____   _____
Signed   Date

You Did It!

_____ **earns this award for**

_____

Keep Up The Great Work!

_____   _____

Signed   Date

Great Job!

_____

Receives this award for

_____

Keep up the great work!

_____   _____
Signed   Date

Great Success!

_____ **earns this award for**

_____

I am Proud of You!

_____ _____
Signed   Date

Congratulations!

_____

Receives this award for

_____

Keep up the great work!

_____   _____
Signed   Date

space suit	splashdown	spoon	Sputnik
stage	star	storage	storm
sun	sunspot	telescope	tiles
Triton	Uranus	Venus	weightless

crystals	dust	earth	eclipse
energy	engine	exercise	experiment
flight deck	float	fuel	galaxy
Galileo	galley	gas	Goddard

gravity	Halley	helium	helmet
hydrogen	inner	Jupiter	laboratory
laika	launch	litter	Mars
Mercury	meteor	meteorite	microgravity

Milky Way	mir	mission	monkey
moon	Neil Armstrong	Neptune	North Star
orbit	outer	oxygen	patch
payload	planet	plastic	Pluto